How to Play

SCRABBLE

Like a

How to Play

Like a

JOEL WAPNICK
World SCRABBLE Champion

PUZZLE
WRIGHT
PRESS

An imprint of Sterling
Publishing Co., Inc.
www.puzzlewright.com

Puzzlewright Press and the distinctive Puzzlewright Press logo
are registered trademarks of Sterling Publishing Co., Inc.

Library of Congress Cataloging-in-Publication Data

Wapnick, Joel.
How to play Scrabble like a champion / by Joel Wapnick.
    p. cm.
"First published in 1986 by Stein and Day, Inc., Scarbororough House,
Briarcliff Manor, NY, as The Champion's Strategy for Winning at Scrabble
Brand Crossword Game."
Includes index.
ISBN 978-1-4027-7077-7 (pbk.)
1. Scrabble (Game) I. Title.

GV1507.S3W37 2010
793.734--dc22
                                        2010022904
10 9 8 7 6 5 4 3 2 1

Published by Sterling Publishing Co., Inc.
387 Park Avenue South, New York, NY 10016
New text © 2010 by Joel Wapnick
First published in 1986 by Stein and Day, Inc., Scarbororough House, Briarcliff Manor,
NY, as *The Champion's Strategy for Winning at SCRABBLE* Brand Crossword Game* and
© 1986 by Joel Wapnick
Distributed in Canada by Sterling Publishing
$^{c}/o$ Canadian Manda Group, 165 Dufferin Street,
Toronto, Ontario, Canada M6K 3H6

Sterling ISBN 978-1-4027-7077-7

For information about custom editions, special sales, premium and
corporate purchases, please contact Sterling Special Sales
Department at 800-805-5489 or specialsales@sterlingpublishing.com.

For Varley

Contents

Acknowledgments

Moses had it easy. He acknowledged the author of those tablets and was done with it. I, on the other hand, did not come down from the mountain with tablets, monoliths, scrolls, podcasts, or anything else resembling commandments for playing a decent game of SCRABBLE. In the beginning I learned from being thrashed by stronger players. Later, some quasi-samizdat publications came to the rescue: Al and Donna Weissman's *Letters for Expert Players*, Brian Sheppard's *Rack Your Brain*, Nick Ballard's *Medleys*, Alan Frank's *Matchups*, Joe Edley's *Tile Rack*, Jim Geary's *JG Newsletter*, and Mark Watson's *Wordgame*.

Although all of these publications contributed to my knowledge of how to play SCRABBLE, *Letters for Expert Players* was the first and most important. Every month we—experts, we called ourselves—were given six SCRABBLE problems to ponder. We chose our best moves, bolstered our choices with attempts at rationality, and mailed them back to Al and Donna the old-fashioned way. Diversity of opinion was the norm. There was much inspired disagreement, which often happens when people grope about and think that they know what they are talking about. Nevertheless, I did learn a few things from the muddle. To the perpetrators of these operations and their contributors—people such as Charles Goldstein, Mike Wise (who died in 1998), Ed Halper, Stephen Fisher, Dan Pratt, Sam Kantimathi, Joe Edley, James Pate, Rich Silberg, Jim Neuberger, Alan Frank, Jeff Reeves, Chris Cree, Robert Felt (who died in 2002), Jeremiah Mead, Peter Morris, Steve Polatnick, and Ron Tiekert—thank you.

I am greatly indebted to Brian Sheppard, and to John O'Laughlin and Jason Katz-Brown for producing two of the strongest-playing computer-based SCRABBLE programs around, Maven and Quackle. Both programs are great learning tools. They can simulate consequences of different moves in a more or less objective way. I used Maven and Quackle to refine my strategic thinking presented in this book. The programs also helped me limit the number of blunders that appear within these pages.

Thanks also to Keith Smith and Seth Lipkin, creators of the SCRABBLE record-keeping website cross-tables.com. Keith and Seth have archived the records of hundreds of championship tournament games on this site, and I have drawn material liberally from them.

I am indebted to Peter Gordon of Puzzlewright Press for choosing to publish this book, for his guidance concerning its direction, and for reformatting all those game diagrams. Deepest thanks also to my expert editor, Hannah Reich, who taught me so much about writing, as well as some secrets of Microsoft Word. Without her help, this book would not have been nearly as good as it is.

Finally, I owe my greatest debt of gratitude to the almost five hundred different opponents I've played in SCRABBLE tournaments over the past years. Thanks, everyone. I couldn't have written this book without you. Nevertheless, don't expect a free copy.

Preface

Though I do not think of myself as an average sort of person, I do concede to being normal in many respects. The proportionality of my horizontal and vertical dimensions approximates normality. I am neither tall nor short. I smile some of the time, not too much and not too little. I am not a Furry. However, there is one way in which I am decidedly not normal. I am a serial preoccupationist.

Preoccupationism is not an unusual characteristic in modern day society. Most people get preoccupied by at least one thing, whether it be another person, an animal, a 40-inch flat-panel television, a Macintosh computer, a ball, a sports car, collecting (think books, movies, CDs, stamps, and coins), gourmet cooking, and so forth. Some of these things have been known to affect me as well, but this is not what makes me unusual. I collect preoccupations. Many of them get milked and abandoned, but a couple have lingered on with me.

I was six years old when I acquired my first preoccupation: license plate recording. I was never a *when are we going to be there?* kind of kid, because I was too preoccupied writing down plate numbers of the cars we passed. I kept my records in a notebook with green graph paper, and I was careful to make sure that each letter or number entered fit securely within its box. I often urged my dad to drive faster so that I could record more licenses.

Six years later I became a numismatist. Nowadays if a kid wants to start a coin collection, he has to go to a coin shop. Back then, you could go forth into the world and collect coins. On Friday nights, my friends Neal and John would go with me to the banking establishments of Lynbrook, New York. We exchanged currency for rolls of nickels, dimes, quarters, and half dollars. After extracting the valuable coins, we rerolled our change and exchanged it for other rolls. Tellers loved us, I'm sure. The climax of the evening involved converting our allowances into rolls of pennies. We then went to one of our houses and spent the next couple of hours eating ice cream and combing through thousands of pennies.

My third preoccupation was the stock exchange, and it took hold of me shortly after my Bar Mitzvah. My approach was to examine the yearly highs and lows of stocks on the New York Stock Exchange. If (1) the current price of a stock was slightly closer to its yearly high than to its yearly low, (2) its high was about 50 percent greater than its low, (3) the stock was not a preferred stock but (4) yielded a substantial dividend, and (5) had a nice name, I was interested. I never made trades—I was thirteen, after all—but I did keep track of how I would have done. I enjoyed reading through all those numbers in *The New York Times* every morning. And I got into some interesting arguments with my father, who was a terrible investor. He lost about a million dollars during the boom years of the '50s and '60s. In 1960 I told him to corner the market on four-dollar U.S. gold pieces known as stellas. But no, he wouldn't listen. If he had, I would be living a life of indolence right now rather than typing away.

Piano playing, which would require another book to do it justice, was my first lifelong preoccupation. Although it is essential to my life, it did not quench my need for additional preoccupations. So when I was twenty-two and quite unhappily enrolled in a graduate psychology program, I became intrigued with horse racing betting systems. I never bet on my systems, which was a good thing. Somewhere in my files I have the rules for the one reliable system I came up with, the only one that came out ahead after more than fifteen races. It was applicable to only one race out of twenty and returned an average profit of a dime for every two dollars bet. Interested?

I took up chess seriously when I was in my mid-twenties. I wasn't great at it. The high point of my chess career came during the 1971 World Open, in New York City. My opponent, whose rating was 300 points higher than mine, appeared to be winning. I made a move and called *check*. Forty-five seconds later, I noticed that *checkmate* was the more appropriate word. I had blundered into a win. That's how good I was.

My mother roped me into a game of SCRABBLE when I was nine years old. I have been playing it ever since, and I have been competing in tournaments since 1975. I suspect that it will remain an important part of my life for the duration. Why this game? I have reserved the first chapter to answer this question. But first I'll tell you something about the history and current popularity of the game.

Alfred Butts, an unemployed American architect, invented what was to become SCRABBLE in 1933. It was first mass marketed in 1949 and became tremendously popular in 1952. This game has retained its phenomenal appeal since then, and not just in North America. SCRABBLE is played worldwide, and in many different languages.

In 1971, the Selchow and Righter Company acquired control of the production and trademark rights to SCRABBLE in North America. Two years later the company established a subsidiary, SCRABBLE Crossword Game Players, to promote SCRABBLE through publication of the SCRABBLE Players News, licensing of SCRABBLE Clubs throughout the United States and Canada, and promotion of SCRABBLE tournaments. Selchow and Righter was also responsible for the publication in 1978 of the Official SCRABBLE Players Dictionary and for the establishment of a unified set of tournament rules.

SCRABBLE was bought by Coleco in the '80s, and was acquired by Milton Bradley, which subsequently became the board games division of Hasbro, Inc. SCRABBLE Crossword Game Players was replaced by the National SCRABBLE Association (NSA), and in 2009 a new entity came into existence to regulate tournament play in North America: the North American SCRABBLE Players Association (NASPA).

Tournament activity in North America has increased steadily over the years. There are now thousands of tournament and club players, and there are over 200 active SCRABBLE clubs throughout the United States and Canada. In 2008, 375 sanctioned tournaments took place, and the National Championship drew 660 players. A World SCRABBLE Championship has been held in the odd-numbered years since 1991. More than 100 players from over 40 countries participated in the 2009 tournament, held in Malaysia.

In view of this pattern of growth, the need for instruction on how to play SCRABBLE has also grown. I wrote this book to meet that need. It is intended for anyone who plays, regardless of ability. It covers all the important strategic elements, from the most basic to the most subtle and elegant. It tells you how to study intelligently in order to improve your game. There are sections dealing in detail with tournament preparation and play. In addition, a major portion of the book is devoted to the analysis of games and exceptional moves played by experts. I guarantee that this book will increase your enjoyment of SCRABBLE by improving your play.

It will also improve your winning percentage, assuming that your opponents do not also read it.

If you are a beginner, don't be scared into thinking that this book is too advanced for you. Although I have presented many aspects of play that you likely have not considered before, there is nothing in here that is beyond comprehension. And while the examples I have used include obscure and unusual words that you probably have not come across before, I cannot see how exposure to them will do anything but increase your playing strength. Many of the extant books dealing with how to play SCRABBLE have not gone beyond the rudiments of the game. The "how-to-play" material in these books is not very challenging and in some cases can easily be summarized in a few pages. Such books teach their readers how to play—poorly. My work also covers rudimentary topics, but it goes beyond them as well. If you are interested enough to read an entire book on how to play SCRABBLE, you will want to play it well. I don't recall ever seeing books in stores with titles such as *Learn Chess from A to B*, or *Six Short Steps to Becoming a Mediocre Bridge Player*. Perhaps someone one day will write *SCRABBLE for Dummies*, but it won't be me.

Notation Conventions

Diagrams

The "address" of any square on a SCRABBLE board can be said to be the intersection of the letters running across the top of a diagram and the numbers running down the left border. The location of a play is indicated by the position of the first letter of the word, expressed as a letter-number combination. When a word is played horizontally, the location is a number followed by a letter; vertical plays are indicated by a letter followed by a number. In the diagram below, APORIA is at 8C, FULLER at A7, and JOSHED at J5.

Shaded squares indicate premium squares. Black squares are triple word squares (A1, for example); squares shaded light gray are double letter squares (A4); medium gray squares are double word squares (3C), and dark gray squares are triple letter squares (6F).

Tiles that appear as outlined letters, such as the B in HOMEBODY at E11, represent blanks.

Racks

A square on the rack symbolizes a blank.

Cappelletto's rack: A C E G I S □

Text

An underlined letter signifies that the letter is a blank.

The other bingos are CAGIEST and INCAGES.

Details of a play are presented in parentheses. The information contained within the parentheses consists of location, score, and, in some cases, cumulative score.

John now threatens both SLATS (M1, 24) and LASS (3E, 15).

The Nature of the Game

A number of Christmases ago, back in the early 1980s, Selchow and Righter's advertising campaign for SCRABBLE consisted mainly of one television commercial that was widely shown across the country. The commercial featured an elegantly dressed handsome, young, white, and apparently heterosexual couple. He was formally attired, and she wore a dazzling evening gown. They arrived home from an exclusive restaurant or perhaps from the theater, in a fancy black luxury car. And now they were facing off across a living room table complete with a burning fireplace in the background and brandy snifters in the foreground. Time to play SCRABBLE! As they gazed at each other with looks that can only be described as lascivious, she effortlessly made the first and only play of the commercial: PANACHE.

The commercial was not repeated in following seasons. Selchow and Righter, in fact, changed advertising agencies shortly after this campaign. There were a number of reasons that the commercial was a failure. The product wasn't adequately displayed, nine-tenths of the viewing audience probably thought that PANACHE was what you got if you ate portions of a pan along with the food on it, and the plotline was absurd. I objected to the commercial on more basic grounds: it wasn't a realistic portrayal of how SCRABBLE is played.

The word *scrabble* means to scratch, grope, or claw about frantically. Real crossword game players scratch their heads a lot.

They make faces, and they grope for the right play. Few plays are effortless, especially plays such as PANACHE. And no matter how charming a man finds a woman, he does not look at her with great longing and excitement immediately after finding himself on the losing end of an 86–0 score. Not if he's a serious player.

The plan of Part I

The chapters in Part I describe what playing SCRABBLE is really like. Chapter 1 is an appreciation. It describes the essence and spirit of the game and it includes some remarkable examples of inspired play. Chapters 2 and 3 deal with the body rather than the soul: rules and words. Chapter 2 presents some obscure rules and it clarifies some others. Chapter 3 describes the Official SCRABBLE Players Dictionary (the OSPD), the bible for most players in North America though not for official club and tournament players, for reasons to be explained later.

Perhaps one day my opponent in a tournament game will be a beautiful brandy-sipping woman dressed in a dazzling evening gown. Perhaps she will begin the game by smiling at me and effortlessly playing some obscure bingo[1] such as MOPOKES or LEKYTHI. If so, I'll smile back, chivalrously refill her glass right up to the rim, and say, "Drink up!"

---

[1] A bingo is a play that uses all seven letters on the rack and is thus worth the value of the play plus 50 points.

CHAPTER 1

SCRABBLE: An Appreciation

My purpose in writing this book is not just to help you improve your play. I also want to increase your appreciation of this marvelous game. Such admiration can be fully developed only by understanding the finesses and complexities in SCRABBLE, which is, simply, the youngest of the great games. I have no doubt that it will continue to be played through the ages.

SCRABBLE is, first and foremost, a word game, and playing with words is a natural form of amusement for many humans. I'm sure that most of you are fascinated with wordplay. For as long as I can remember, I have taken words apart in my head, rearranged the letters variously, spelled them in reverse, and attempted to find shorter words within longer ones. If you like doing these things, you will love SCRABBLE.

Second, SCRABBLE requires creativity and imagination. The player who looks for the unexpected will be rewarded often. Most of us enjoy experiencing a eureka phenomenon. In SCRABBLE, this can occur in a variety of ways. The player may discover an unusual or unlikely word, or may make five new words on one play, or may uncover hidden resources in the board position, or may even make a move that looks mundane but actually is strategically brilliant.

	A	B	C	D	E	F	G	H	I	J	K	L	M	N	O
1						H	E	A	L						
2		B	E	D	S	O	N	I	A						
3			E												
4			L						I						
5			I		C		M	O	V	I	N	G			
6			Q		E						S				
7			U		I		B				I				
8	W	H	O	R	L		P	U	T	Z		D	A	M	P
9			R		I			L	A	N	E				
10				N			K		G	O	R				
11	W				G	R	E	Y			U				
12	I	V	I	E	S						N	A			C
13	T	O									A	N			O
14	E	X								F	L	Y	T	E	D
15	D				R	E	T	I	A						A

Nigel Richards's rack: A E O R S T U
Robert Felt's rack: E F J O T

This position was reached in a game played at the 2002 National SCRABBLE Championship. The game was between two champions, Nigel Richards and Robert Felt. Both racks are given because the game is nearly over. The bag was empty, and Robert only had five tiles on his rack. It was Nigel's turn, and he found a play that both scored well and retained tiles so that he could play out on his next turn—an important advantage, as the first person to play away all his tiles gets double the value of the tiles remaining on his opponent's rack added to his score.

Nigel played SANE (10C, 29). With his remaining four tiles, ORTU, he was able to play ROQUET (6A, 19) on his next turn. Exquisite!

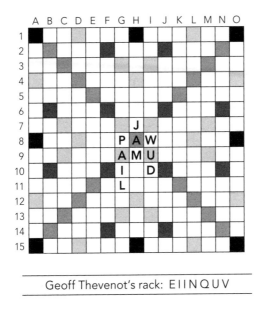

Geoff Thevenot's rack: E I I N Q U V

In this game from the 2008 Dallas Open, Geoff Thevenot played away his U even though a Q remained on his rack. In order to solve this one, you need to know that QI is an acceptable word. Geoff played UNVEIL (11B, 18), which both set up a Q play at 10F (QI, 62) and created a huge QU possibility at B10. He played QI on his next turn.

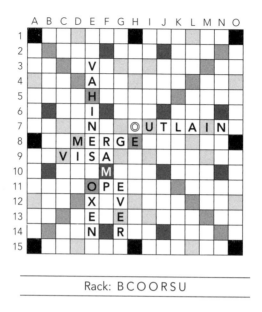

Rack: B C O O R S U

Here is an example of a brilliant play that does not involve thinking ahead to the following move: MICROBUS (D8, 60). The play is unusual because it extends the MI already on the board, and because it creates four words besides itself: ROPE, OX, BE, and UN.

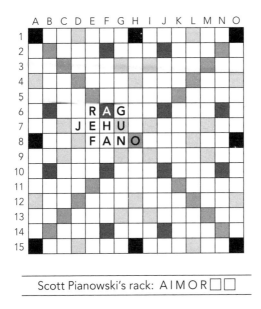

Scott Pianowski's rack: A I M O R ☐ ☐

Here is another example of a word extension, played by Scott Pianowski. The neat thing about this play is that the word was extended in *both* directions to cover two double word squares and score 102 points: A<u>NT</u>IREFORM (E2)! OM<u>NIV</u>ORA (H8) is nice, but A<u>NT</u>IREFORM is brilliant.

As creative as these examples are, they represent only one aspect of SCRABBLE. They are instances of brilliant tactical plays or short-term stratagems rather than of strategic planning. Thanks to a number of resources, strategic theory has developed greatly over the past few years. We shall see later that the implementation of sound strategy requires at least as much creativity as does the ability to find tactical brilliancies.

And then there's luck. That there is a significant element of chance in what is essentially a game of skill sometimes works in my favor, of course—but as a skilled player, I find this aspect infuriating. SCRABBLE expertise can be achieved through playing experience and study. Due to the chance factor, however, performance always will be partially beyond the control of even the most accomplished player. Strong players must therefore play as well as they can to minimize the number of upsets pulled against them by weaker players. In addition, players who wish to improve must develop the self-awareness to distinguish their own weak play from chance. It is very easy to blame the tiles for a losing effort. More often than not, the fault is not in our tiles, but in ourselves.

Another attraction of SCRABBLE is that it is aesthetically pleasing. The board, with its intricate pattern of differently hued colors, is lovely. The tiles have a nice smooth feel, and all the varieties of them that I possess (consisting of various combinations of white, blue, maroon, violet, silver, and black letterings and backgrounds) are very attractive. The geometrical designs of the tiles on the board often are intriguing.

Finally, I like the fast pace of the game. Unlike some other recreational activities of consenting adults, the enjoyment derived from playing SCRABBLE is inversely related to its duration. There is nothing quite so frustrating as waiting fifteen minutes for an opponent to play CAT for 10 points. Fortunately, strict time limitations are observed in sanctioned club and tournament games. These limitations do affect the quality of play. It is very difficult to play a perfect game under time constraints. Experienced players expect that they will make mistakes and that the "credit" for some of their victories will belong to their opponents' blunders. They know that the winner of a game is usually the person who makes fewer mistakes. However, they are willing to put up with the consequences of a clocked game in order to experience the excitement, tension, and anxiety that builds up during the course of a close game. I find that even though these feelings interfere with my concentration over the board, I am glad to have them, for they help make this game as absorbing and challenging as it is. Want to feel alive? Play tournament SCRABBLE.

Leonard Bernstein once wrote that no other activity gave him as much satisfaction as the act of composing—not drinking that first glass of orange juice in the morning, nor making love. SCRABBLE may not afford you the satisfaction that any of the above activities might. On the other hand . . .

CHAPTER 2

Rules

TIME: 9:30 pm Tuesday, August 9, 1983.
PLACE: A meeting room in the Drake Hotel, Chicago.
PARTICIPANTS: The thirty-two players who qualified to take part in the
North American SCRABBLE Championship, beginning the next day;
and Jim Houle, president of SCRABBLE Crossword Game Players and
tournament director of the North American Championship.
PURPOSE: Clarification of the rules.

I remember this meeting very well. A reception for the players had just ended.
The reception featured the presence of Alfred Butts, inventor of SCRABBLE,
and the unveiling of the tournament trophy. Selchow and Righter had
commissioned sculptor Milton Sherrill to create the trophy, which according to
the SCRABBLE Players News was "a semiabstract S depicting the spirit of the
classic board game." It was a handsome work, and if you looked closely at some
of the players at its unveiling, you could see them salivating at the prospect of
winning it. Another feature of the reception was the consumption of a good
deal of alcohol. Anticipation of the tournament had made a number of the
competitors tense, and it had occurred to several of them to drink their way
to relaxation. I was hoping to play them the next morning.

   The meeting was adversarial. Players disagreed among themselves and
with Jim Houle. People constantly were being interrupted. Voices were loud

and confrontational. Here were thirty-two of the most rules-knowledgeable players in the country, most of whom had played in tournaments for years, arguing ferociously over the rules. How could this be? Didn't they know the rules by now?

Of course they knew the basic rules. This game is very complex, however. Not all contingencies of play are covered by the instructions included with each game. In addition, expert players have vivid imaginations. They are great at imagining ways in which rules might be legally but unscrupulously bent by their opponents.

I wish that I could report, twenty-seven years later, that the rules of SCRABBLE have been set in stone. They haven't, and probably never will be. Rules keep getting added. They deal with such things as how to draw tiles out of the bag (with the bag at eye level, eyes averted), the proper way to designate the blank as representing a letter, the precise moment when a turn ends, and how one goes about putting one's hand in the bag to count tiles (show an open palm to the opponent first). The rule book is also plagued with the word *may*, which doesn't belong in a rule book.

The purpose of this chapter is to clarify some of the more obscure rules of the game. I am assuming that you know the rudiments. If you do not, please read Appendix B, which describes the physical dimensions of SCRABBLE (board, racks, and tiles). It also tells you how to begin a game, how to make legal plays, and how to calculate your score. The section you are reading now deals with virtually everything else and is geared toward club and tournament play. The official tourney rules are available from the North American SCRABBLE Players Association (NASPA), and an accurate presentation of them can be found online at the NASPA website (see Appendix A).

Scoring

Some aspects of scoring may not be clear to the casual player. Tie games are one example. Until the late 1970s, ties were broken on the basis of the single-highest-scoring play in the game. Whoever made that play was the winner. This is no longer the case. There are no tiebreakers. A tie is a tie, and in a tournament it counts as half a win and half a loss.

The scoring at the end of the game, though unambiguously stated in the rules, is sometimes misunderstood. A player is said to play out when she makes a play that uses all the tiles on her rack and there are no replacement tiles left in the bag. Such a play ends the game. The player who plays out gets a bonus: twice the total value of the tiles on her opponent's rack is added to her score.

It occasionally happens that because of unwieldy tiles on the rack or a constricted board position, neither player can play out. In such a case, the total value of each player's tiles remaining on the racks is deducted from their respective scores. If I am stuck with a V and my opponent is stuck with a Q, 4 points are deducted from my score and 10 points are deducted from my opponent's score.

There is no point bonus for winning a game. In the early days of tournament playing, a 50-point cushion was awarded to the game winner. This was done to prevent collusion on the part of the players, both of whom under the rules at that time stood to benefit from high scores rather than from winning games. A player's tournament standing nowadays depends primarily on won-lost record, so a 50-point bonus for winning is unnecessary.

Checking the tile distribution

In a tournament, you should always check the tile distribution of the set you are using before beginning each and every game. It is your option to check for the correct number of tiles for each letter, but in practice this is done only at the beginning of the day. Nevertheless, after verifying that there are one hundred tiles in the set, I usually look around to make sure that there are two blanks, four S's, and one each of the J, Q, X, and Z. If an incorrect distribution is discovered after the game has begun, the players have no recourse. They are stuck with the tiles in their bag, even if they include five Q's and two U's.

The tile distribution can become fouled up if two games are played at the same table and a player inadvertently picks tiles from the wrong bag. This happens fairly frequently with novices and intermediates and is a tournament director's nightmare. A cheater can of course deliberately foul up the distribution by pocketing some of the more desirable tiles from a set for the next game. It happens, but fortunately very rarely.

Picking tiles from the bag

According to the rules, tiles can be picked one at a time, put facedown on the table in front of the rack, and then placed on the rack. Also acceptable is to hold the bag with one hand at arm's length and at eye level, and with eyes averted, to withdraw tiles with the other hand, taking as many at a time as is comfortable. The tiles are then placed directly on the rack. Today's tournament players use tiles that cannot be brailled. (In other words, you cannot feel the letters with your fingertips to determine what you're drawing from the bag. In the old days, a tile that felt smooth was more likely to be a blank than one that didn't.) So you need not worry about being accused of cheating if you are slow in getting the tiles out of the bag.

It sometimes happens that a player will accidentally pick an extra replacement tile or two. The rule for handling this situation is as follows: if the replacement tiles have been put on the rack, the opponent picks $x + 2$ tiles from the player's rack, where x = the number of overdrawn tiles. For example, imagine that a player plays away three tiles and then draws four from the bag. His opponent would then choose three tiles from the eight to look at. He would then return the tile of his choice into the bag and the other two to the player. If the replacement tiles have not been put on the rack, the opponent picks only from those tiles. In the particular case of drawing two tiles when one should have been drawn, and those tiles have not been placed on the rack, the opponent looks only at the two tiles and selects one, which he returns to the bag. The moral of the story is to be very careful not to pick excess tiles when you hold the blank, or else you may lose it! It's happened to me twice in tournament games.

Time limitations

All tournament games require competitors to adhere to time constraints. This has resulted in the adoption of chess clocks for tournament and club play. There are manufacturers who make digital clocks that are particularly suited for SCRABBLE. For the uninitiated, a chess clock is a more or less rectangular box that houses two clock faces. Two buttons protrude from the top casing, one directly above each of the clock readouts. When the button above one of the two clocks is depressed, the clock beneath it stops. At the same time, the other button is propelled upward and the opponent's clock begins ticking.

Correct procedure for using the chess clock is simple. The clocks are set to 25 minutes for each player. Once the player who goes first has seen one of his seven tiles, the opponent presses the button on his side of the clock, which starts the first player's clock. After the first player has made a play and announces her score, she presses her clock button. It is incorrect to push the button before announcing one's score. She then records her score for the play and her cumulative score for the game, and only after doing so picks replacement tiles from the bag. The penalty for exceeding the time limit is 10 points subtracted from the player's score for each excess minute or fraction thereof.

The sequence of forming a word, announcing the score, depressing the clock button, recording the score, and selecting replacement tiles from the bag is repeated after every succeeding move in the game. It is the player's responsibility to remember to depress the clock button after making a play.

It used to be that if there was a break in the action (during a challenge, when a player detects an addition mistake, or when a player leaves the table for some reason), the buttons were adjusted so that neither clock was running. This is currently the case for challenging and correcting scoring errors. If a player must leave the table, however, she must do so after making a play but before replenishing her rack. Her opponent may play at any time and then depress the clock. The opponent cannot replenish his rack until she returns, and time on her clock will tick off in her absence.

Challenges

A challenge results in the loss of a turn. If the word in question is ruled acceptable, the challenger loses the turn. If the word is unacceptable, the person who has been challenged removes her tiles from the board, receives no points, and forfeits her turn. In order to be ruled acceptable, the word in question need be in the official lexicon. The player whose word is challenged does not have to define her challenged word. Nowadays, it is rare to have a word judge come to the playing table. Instead, the two players place their tiles facedown on the table and then walk to a computer station. Word adjudication is done by a software program called Zyzzyva, developed by Michael Thelen.

Bluffing is part of the game. If a player plays a phony word and his opponent does not challenge it, the word stays on the board, and the player adds to his score however many points the play is worth. If there are no computer stations at a tournament, an official word judge rather than one of the players should consult the word source to determine a challenged word's legality, as information found by looking up the word might affect future play. An opponent once played ARRASES, which I challenged. No one else was present, so I had to look it up. I saw that ARRASES was a phony,[2] but could not avoid noticing that ARRASED was acceptable. That was useful to know should my opponent try to play ARRASED on his next turn. If my opponent had looked up ARRASES, his newly gained knowledge of ARRASED might have posed an ethical dilemma for him on his next turn.

There are a number of procedural niceties associated with challenging. One challenges by verbal declaration. This should be done only after the player challenged has depressed the button on his clock, officially ending his turn, but before he has replenished his rack with tiles from the bag. If a player challenges after the word is placed on the board and the score is tallied, but before his opponent depresses the clock button, his opponent has the right to withdraw the word and make a different play if he so wishes. There is a gray area here, for the challenger's reminder to his opponent to press his clock button may tip off his opponent that a challenge is imminent. Purposefully refraining from pressing the clock button in order to see if an opponent will challenge is of course unethical. The correct way to handle such behavior is to call over the tournament director.

This situation raises the question of whether a player should inform the opponent that the opponent has neglected to press the clock button after making a play. A player could refrain from making a move until after the opponent notices the oversight. This would cost the opponent valuable time. The rules in fact specify that it is not the player's responsibility to inform the opponent of the failure to press the clock button. Nevertheless, I would not want to win a game in this way. I always inform my opponents if they have forgotten to press their clock buttons, except if they forget repeatedly. Then they are on their own.

---

[2] It isn't any more. ARRASES was added to the OSPD in 2006.

A prospective challenger need not challenge immediately after her opponent makes his play. She may instead declare "hold." Once she does this, her opponent cannot pick tiles from the bag. The prospective challenger considers whether to challenge or not on her own time, however, as her opponent has already pressed his clock button.

The decision to challenge or not to challenge often depends on a number of factors and may be very difficult to make. It is thus in the interest of maximizing best play to allow the prospective challenger as much time as she needs to come to a decision. The only problem with allowing unlimited time for challenging is that the player who made the play that may be challenged must wait during this interval without seeing his new tiles. A player who thus routinely declares "hold" after every move would be depriving her opponent of the opportunity to formulate moves during the time she is deliberating whether or not to challenge. In order to deal with this problem, a rule was adopted that allows the opponent unlimited time to challenge after calling "hold." However, the player who may be challenged can draw replacement tiles after waiting for one minute. These tiles are kept separate from the tiles remaining on his rack. If the play is challenged successfully, the replacement tiles go back in the bag after both players have seen them.

If a play creates two or more new words, the challenger has the right to challenge all the new words at the same time. The play is ruled unacceptable if any one of the words challenged is phony. In such a case, the players are informed that the whole play is unacceptable; they receive no knowledge concerning which of the words challenged are good and which are not. They know for sure only that at least one of the words must be unacceptable.

There is no penalty for challenging the last play of the game. If your opponent plays out and you are even slightly unsure whether the play is acceptable, you should challenge. Similarly, there is no penalty for challenging more than one new word formed on a given play versus simply challenging one word. The challenge to the additional words can thus also be regarded as "free" challenges.

Exchanging and passing tiles

As long as there are at least seven tiles remaining in the bag, a player may exchange any or all of the tiles on his rack for new ones. He simply announces "I exchange x [a number from one to seven] tiles," places the tiles to be exchanged facedown on the table, depresses his clock button, picks the replacement tiles from the bag and places them on his rack, and returns the tiles on the table to the bag. He receives no points for exchanging. There is no limit to the number of times that a player is allowed to exchange tiles during a game.

Passing consists of forfeiting a turn without tile replacement. The player announces "I pass" and then presses her clock button. A player may pass at any time during the game. Sometimes a player must pass. This happens when there are fewer than seven tiles in the bag and the player is unable to make a legal play. We shall see that there are times when it is advantageous for a player to pass, even though it is not necessary to do so.

Ending the game by repeated passing and/or exchanging

After six exchanges or passes in a row (three plays of either type by each player), either player may terminate the game simply by declaring the game to be over. The total value of the tiles on the players' racks is then subtracted from their respective scores, and a winner is determined. If neither player declares the game over, play continues.

In order for the game to end in this manner, at least one word must have been played on the board. It must stay there and score at least one point. Successfully challenged phonies don't count, nor do two-letter words played with both blanks (!).

Tournament pairings

Most tournaments use a modified Swiss system for determining pairings. Pairings are made on the basis of similar won-lost records. If after five rounds you have won three games, you are likely to play someone next who also has won three games. Point-spread differentials (the total number of points scored by a player in the tournament minus the total number of points scored against that player) are used to break ties.

Other lands, other rules

There are some major rules differences between the way SCRABBLE is played in North America and the way it is played elsewhere. Tournaments held in the French-speaking world (including Quebec) emphasize fairness. Their game is called *le SCRABBLE Duplicate*. Players sit alone at tables and do not play against each other. Instead, a master board is set up at the front of the room. A tournament official selects seven oversized tiles and places them where they can be easily seen by everyone in the room. The players then have three minutes to come up with the highest scoring play they can find. This is the sole criterion of excellence. Each player gets credit for the number of points earned (a player gets no points for playing a phony word), and the highest scoring play found by any of the players is added to the board. A tournament official then picks replacement tiles, and the game continues until the tiles are used up.

I find this a sterile way of playing SCRABBLE. The chance factor is removed, but so are all of the lovely strategic considerations. *Le SCRABBLE Duplicate* is to North American English SCRABBLE what a foul-shooting contest is to basketball.

In Great Britain and in a number of other countries, SCRABBLE is much closer to North American style play than it is to French play in that the games consist of contests between two players. The only significant rules difference is that there is no penalty for challenging a questionable word that turns out to be acceptable.

I dislike this elimination of bluffing. I have heard people describe the purposeful playing of phonies as dishonest, unaesthetic, and a form of cheating. I could not disagree more. Bluffing is as inherent to SCRABBLE as it is to poker. It places the greatest possible burden on the players to know their words. In a game with a significant luck factor, bluffing is one more tool that the expert player can use in order to win a game. The proper playing of phonies is a skill rather than an accident. It requires cleverness, imagination, and good timing.

This does not mean that it is always proper to try to win by bluffing. In a tournament game, I would feel no compunction about playing phonies whenever I thought that playing them would help me win. In club and informal play, however, it is unconscionable to play intentional phonies for the express purpose of rolling up the score against an obviously weaker player.

Upside-down plays

Let us end this rather sober chapter with some silliness. A number of years ago the SCRABBLE Players News reported on a game in which one of the players placed an upside-down word on the board. It was a vertically played word, and its letters were facing in the direction opposite the direction in which all of the other vertical words on the board were facing. Believe it or not, this game was played between two experts! The word was not challenged and wasn't noticed by either player until a turn or two later in the game. The ruling from SCRABBLE Central was that the upside-down word had to come off the board. The game would revert to the point at which this play was made, and the player who made the word would lose her turn. This ruling struck many players as incorrect. A more logical approach would have been to consider that the player had simply placed her individual letters on the board upside down. Some players do this routinely with O's, N's, S's, and so forth. The letters look the same as when they are correctly placed, but the tile values are upside down—in the upper left-hand corner rather than right-side-up in the lower right-hand corner. An upside down play of BLOCK for example is really KCOLB. If the opponent challenges upside-down BLOCK, he should write KCOLB on the challenge sheet.

There are some interesting implications of this interpretation. If, for example, one player plays CARES upside down, her opponent might challenge SERAC—a legal word. The challenger would lose the challenge, though she presumably would have the right to turn the upside-down tiles right-side-up— if she so desired.

There is also the issue of what happens if the first word of a game is played upside down relative to the letterings on the premium squares—that is, the squares that are colored to indicate double and triple letter and word values. Due to the fact that the board is symmetrical, neither player may notice that all or almost all of the words on the board are phonies! One player could conceivably challenge BOX in the middle of such a game, claiming that the word just played is not BOX but XOB. I assume that most rational tournament directors would, in this circumstance, consider the orientation of the lettering on the premium squares to be irrelevant to the game.

Enough of this. Let's move on to the real rules of SCRABBLE—the words!

CHAPTER 3

Words

The rules booklet included in every SCRABBLE set contains a sample game. The first eight words formed in this game are HORN, FARM, PASTE, MOB, DIAL, PREVENT, MODELS, and QUITE. Expert players sometimes play common words like these, but about half the time they play words that are unfamiliar to the casual player. Some of the words played by Joe Edley and me in just one tournament game were AGLEY, BIAXAL, VAHINE, QUATE, POGONIAS, GARRON, RECK, PEISED, FON, MHO, and LINTEL.

The Official SCRABBLE Players Dictionary

Once upon a time, there used to be two official dictionaries for SCRABBLE play: the *Official SCRABBLE Players Dictionary* (henceforth referred to as the OSPD), for words up to eight letters in length, and *Merriam-Webster's Collegiate Dictionary*, for words from nine to fifteen letters long (both published by Merriam-Webster). In the mid-1990s, however, Hasbro modified the OSPD by eliminating words from it that were considered obscene or might be interpreted as racial or ethnic slurs. Currently, there are more than three hundred such words. Tournament players protested vigorously, and the result was a compromise. *The Official Tournament and Club Word List* (OWL) is used in tournament and SCRABBLE club play, and the OSPD is recommended for use by everyone else. The OWL is not censored and is not sold in bookstores; one must be a member of the North American SCRABBLE Players Association in order to purchase it. The book you are reading applies both to the OSPD and to the OWL, as I have selected board positions and games that do not require consideration of words from the dark side.

It is important to remember that the OSPD was developed for SCRABBLE play. It is not an all-purpose dictionary. You will find no pronunciation guides or etymologies within it. There is only one definition per word, and these definitions are brief. Moreover, hundreds of them are identical, e.g., "a mineral." If you really want to know a word's meaning, look it up somewhere else. The OSPD's one sterling quality is that it is unambiguous. A challenged word is either in the dictionary or it is not. There are no gray areas. The OSPD includes all acceptable conjugations and noun plurals. It specifies which adjectives take -IER and -IEST and which do not. It tells you when it is permissible to tack an S onto a word ending in -ING. The *Funk and Wagnall Standard College Dictionary*, which was the official tournament dictionary before the OSPD was first published back in 1978, did not always specify these things, and neither do other dictionaries. In short, the OSPD leaves no room for subjective interpretations. If LONGSHOT isn't in the OSPD (and it isn't) and is challenged, it will always be taken off the board.

The latest edition of the OSPD contains about 84,000 two- to eight-letter entries. Most people have a vocabulary that is only a small fraction of this number. A good club and tournament player might know nine-tenths of the words. Top players are familiar with all but a few dozen, and a very few players know them all.

As we shall soon see, the OSPD contains some bizarre words. Some of these may strike you as ridiculous, absurd, improper, obscure, or incorrect. Some of them certainly seem that way to me. Nevertheless, try not to be too much of a language chauvinist. All of the words in the OSPD supposedly appeared earlier in at least two of five respected American collegiate dictionaries. Lexicographers are responsible for these words, not crazed fanatics who try to shove the linguistic equivalent of the kitchen sink into the OSPD.

Words of foreign origin

Foreign words are not allowable in SCRABBLE. However, it is difficult to distinguish between a foreign word and a word of foreign origin that has become part of the North American English language. The OSPD is filled with words of foreign origin reflecting the fact that both Canada and the U.S. are cultural melting pots. Here are some examples: JOEY, COOEE; ZITI, LINGUINI, MAFIA, PAISAN; ZAFTIG, ZOFTIG, GONIF, SCHLEPP, SCHLOCK; GOR, BEGORRAH, GAE, GORSE, MUN, WAE; COUTEAU, ROUSSEAU, EAU, MONSIEUR, CHEZ; HAJ, DJIN, IMAM, JIHAD, HAFIZ; YOM, EPHAH, HAZAN, KIBBUTZ; HAIKU, DOJO, NISEI, ISSEI, KAMIKAZE, SUMO; ZARZUELA, JEFE, JIPIJAPA, JOTA, GAZPACHO, LLANO, PAMPA; SAHIB, MEMSAHIB, SUTRA, SUTTEE, DHARMA, DHARNA, DHOLE, DHOTI; OUZO, BOUZOUKI, ILIAD, NOMOS, EXODOI; MOUJIK, KULAK, KOLKHOZ, PIROG; WOK, YIN, YANG; ANGST, STREUSEL, FUEHRER, NAZI, FRAULEIN; BWANA, MBIRA, MAKUTA; and FJORD, SKIJORER, TELEMARK.

Some of these words may strike you as exclusively foreign rather than of foreign origin. The creators of the OSPD did not concern themselves with this distinction. The only criterion for a word's inclusion was whether or not it made it into at least two of the collegiate dictionaries consulted. And yes, there are plenty of inconsistencies. FEMME is allowable, but HOMME is not.

Prefixes and suffixes

Prefixes and suffixes figure in thousands of OSPD words. This is not surprising, but some of the specific words are. Here are some rather unusual inclusions: BEBLOOD, BECHALK, BEDIAPER, BEFINGER, BEUNCLED, DENUDER, ENDAMAGE, MISMEET, MISTRYST, NONEGO, OUTCHIDE, OUTECHO, OUTFROWN, OUTGNAW, OUTHOWL, OUTPLOD, OUTSNORE, OUTSULK, OUTYELP, OVERCOY, OVERFAT, OVERFOUL, OVERHOLY, OVERMEEK, OVERPERT, OVERSUP, SEMIHOBO, SUBSHRUB, BIDEABLE, TAKEABLE, GIVEABLE, DOGDOM, MOVIEDOM, SODALESS, LORNNESS,

LOSTNESS, SISSIEST, and SELFWARD. Among my favorites are unusual nouns ending in -ER such as PREFACER, OUTLIVER, VOMITER, PRELUDER, and SUBSIDER.

There are two special lists in the OSPD. One presents RE- verbs, and the other shows UN- adjectives and adverbs. Some choice entries from these lists are RECLASP, REEJECT, REPLUNGE, RESTUFF, REUTTER, UNCHEWED, UNCLOYED, UNCOMELY, UNFUSSY, UNHOLILY, UNSPRUNG, and UNWRUNG. It pays to know these lists.

Exclamations and utterances

The OSPD contains an admirably expressive collection of exclamations, oaths, utterances, and vocalizations. Among them are AHA, OCHONE, HUH, OHO, PHT, PSST, GOR, PHPHT, RAH, SH, SHH, NERTS, NERTZ, OW, WHEE, PFUI, PHEW, PUGH, and ZOWIE. Naturally, none of these words can be pluralized. You should be aware, however, that certain words appearing to be exclamations are actually verbs, and thus can be both conjugated and pluralized. These include AAH, OH, TSK, TSKTSK, HUMPH, and PSHAW. In addition, there are at least two nouns that are more commonly thought of as exclamations: UGH and HAH. UGHS sounds strange, but it's in the book.

"Poor" English, slang, and "shorthand" words

The OSPD includes words such as ET, FORGAT, AFEARED, ITHER and YEAH. It also includes "shorthand" words such as LEGIT (a noun), INFO, AMMO, AWOL, EXEC, NUDIE, NUKE, BIO, BOD, TRAD, UMP, FESS (meaning to confess), LOOIE and LOUIE (short for lieutenant), and DEMO. A MAXI is a type of dress or coat, and a MINI is "something distinctively smaller than others of its kind." ELHI means "pertaining to school grades 1 through 12" (elementary-high school).

Among the many other slang or near-slang words are FED (a federal agent) and GAY (they are both nouns), LULU ("something remarkable"), JOHN, HOMO, FROSH, ADMAN, BROMO, YACK, and YUK.

Unusual spellings and strange comparative forms

The OSPD contains a considerable number of variant spellings that may strike you as incorrect. Some examples are DANDRIFF, DROWND, PASTROMI, VITAMINE, BROCOLI, and SURVIVER. It also includes bizarre comparatives such as UNIQUER, PERFECTER, ABSOLUTER, DOGGONEDER, GLADLIER, WINSOMER, UNRIPER, UNHANDIER, and UNIFORMER. The number of these words is fortunately small. If more were included, the OSPD would be an even "unusualer" book than it already is.

Unexpected, irregular, and inconsistent pluralizations

There are a considerable number of words in the OSPD that appear to be adjectives but are nouns as well. They can be pluralized. The OSPD thus includes words such as IMMATURES, ADAMANTS, ECSTATICS, RAWS, OLDS, NEEDFULS, UNWASHEDS, MERES, and BIZARRES. I would like to say that these words are bizarres, but that would be incorrect—a bizarre is a kind of flower. There are many, many more of these unexpected pluralizations in the OSPD.

Occasionally a word that appears to be a past tense is also a noun. A TORE is "a large convex molding." A CAME is a window rod, and a STANK is a pond. A LAMED is a Hebrew letter. You may draw a challenge by tacking an S onto any of these words, so it pays to know them and others like them.

You should also be aware that many nouns with S's tacked onto them are allowable even though they may not seem quite right. I am thinking of words such as DEADS, OVERMUCHES, MUCHNESSES, TWOFOLDS, TENFOLDS, TENNISES and OXYGENS. My favorite is TRECENTOS. Its OSPD definition is "the fourteenth century." The plural allows for parallel universes, I suppose.

The OSPD is also a minefield of irregular and inconsistent pluralizations. When experts play weaker players, they often play words that take irregular pluralizations on purpose, even if a slightly stronger but less deceptive play is available. This creates an opportunity for their opponents to lose a turn by incorrectly pluralizing these words, or by incorrectly challenging the experts' correct pluralizations. They may also fail to challenge experts' incorrect pluralizations. The following discussion will give you an idea of how varied and confusing pluralizations can be.

Sometimes a pluralization does not alter the word (CATTLE, RENMINBI, NGWEE). At other times, the pluralization is irregular. A number of words are pluralized by adding E only (BACCA/BACCAE, MUSCA/MUSCAE, APHTHA/APHTHAE). Others take either E or S (AMEBA/AMEBAE/ AMEBAS, LAMINA/LAMINAE/LAMINAS, PATINA/PATINAE/ PATINAS). Some words sound as if they should obey the same rules but don't. For example, QUAICHS and QUAICHES are acceptable plurals of QUAICH, but LAICHS (and not LAICHES) is the only plural of LAICH.

Words ending in -US are sometimes pluralized with an I only (ACINUS/ ACINI, ACARUS/ACARI); sometimes with -USES only (HIATUS/ HIATUSES); sometimes with either -I or -US (PAPYRUS/PAPYRI/ PAPYRUSES); and sometimes with neither (the plural of CANTUS is CANTUS). Similarly, although singular nouns ending with a Y are most often pluralized by dropping the Y and adding -IES in its place, a few allow -YS as well as -IES (SHINDY/SHINDYS/SHINDIES, HENRY/HENRYS/HENRIES). Others allow only the -YS ending (BENDY/BENDYS, BLUEY/BLUEYS).

These examples only scratch the surface. Words can be pluralized by adding -IM (BAAL/BAALIM), -Y (GROSZ/GROSZY), -EN (AUTOBAHN/ AUTOBAHNEN), -TA (BEMA/BEMATA), -U (HALER/HALERU), -I (DJINN/DJINNI), -R (KRONE/KRONER), -N (SCHUL/SCHULN); by replacing -OS with -OI (NOMOS/NOMOI; EXODOS/EXODOI), -F with -VES (TURF/TURVES; CORF/CORVES), -X with -CES (CALX/ CALCES), -IUM with -IA (CORIUM/CORIA), -S with -NTES (ATLAS/ ATLANTES), -S with -DES (OTITIS/OTITIDES), -A with -Y (KORUNA/ KORUNY), et cetera, et cetera. Sometimes plurals are only remotely related to their singular forms (LIKUTA-MAKUTA), at least from the perspective of one unfamiliar with the origins of these words. Additional confusion results from the fact that some but not all words with irregular pluralizations can also be pluralized with -S.

The OSPD is not consistent in its pluralizations of similar words. For example, SFORZANDO and SFUMATO are both listed as nouns in the OSPD. SFORZANDO's plurals are SFORZANDOS and SFORZANDI, but SFUMATI is a phony—the only plural of SFUMATO is SFUMATOS. Similarly, MUNGOOSE is given as an alternate spelling of MONGOOSE. Both words take -S plurals, but though MONGEESE is an acceptable alternative pluralization of MONGOOSE, MUNGEESE is a phony. ENOSISES and NOESISES are both allowable, but DIESISES isn't.

Finally, you should be aware that many words appearing to be pluralizable by adding -S are not. I consider knowledge of these words so important that I study them thoroughly before every tournament I play in. I also try to play them against weaker players, in the hope that I might win a challenge should they attempt to hook an -S onto them. Some examples of these words are AVA, FEY, GEY, MIM, VEG, WUD, CORF, LEVA, SYBO, VITA, YELD, ALGID, KRONA, LYARD, PELON, and VOGIE. There are hundreds more.

Other OSPD inconsistencies

The OSPD's inconsistencies are infuriating at first, but they become weapons once they are learned. Some examples are: INSOFAR is acceptable, INASMUCH is not; though INQUIRE and ENQUIRE are both good, INQUIRER is acceptable and ENQUIRER is not; FIXT, MIXT, UNFIXT, UNMIXT, and REMIXT are good, but REFIXT, OVERMIXT, and INTERMIXT are phonies; LOUDLIER is good, SOFTLIER is not; TIMIDEST is okay, but RIGIDEST isn't (play RIDGIEST instead); COLOR, COLOUR, and RECOLOR are fine, but RECOLOUR is phony; and AXLIKE is acceptable but AXELIKE is not.

In summary, the two most notable characteristics of the OSPD are that (1) it is permissive in that it includes many words of foreign origin, unusual applications of prefixes and suffixes, exclamations (some of which are even listed as verbs or nouns), examples of "poor" English, slang, strange spellings and comparative forms, and otherwise unusual pluralizations; and that (2) it is often internally inconsistent with respect to the ways in which similar words are dealt with. Both characteristics increase the challenge for the serious

SCRABBLE player. The OSPD's permissiveness means that there are more words to learn, and its inconsistency means that it's easy to get confused. I wouldn't want it any other way.

SCRABBLE, word study, vocabulary, and educational benefits

SCRABBLE can easily be thought of as an educational endeavor. The rapid growth of school SCRABBLE in Thailand and Malaysia, for example, has been due in no small measure to assertions that SCRABBLE is an effective way to learn English. And on the North American school SCRABBLE website, one finds the following quotation: *SCRABBLE is a great learning tool, and . . . it is an excellent opportunity for students to improve their reading, math and spatial skills all while having fun.*

I don't deny these claims. Nevertheless, it is important to understand that we are talking about a game here. Sure, we can learn something about mechanical physics from bowling, or acoustics from music, or even physiology, biology, and anatomy from lovemaking. But that's hardly the point.

Experts take SCRABBLE seriously because they love the game. We study words to improve our play. Sometimes we do study definitions, but we learn them in order to help us remember the words. SCRABBLE may not teach us all that much about word meanings, but who cares? Does javelin throwing keep the enemy away or put food on the table? We play games and sports because we like them, not because they are useful or educational. Actually, many SCRABBLE experts do know the definitions of the strange words they play. I have sometimes seen them at tournaments conversing in what seems like a code, until I realize that this code is in fact the English language.

It has been suggested that SCRABBLE players be required to define any challenged words. There are problems with this suggestion. First, the adequacy of a definition may be a matter of sharp dispute. Is the OSPD definition of "a mineral" good enough for QUARTZ and for GARNET? If so, why not get even more general and allow "a thing" instead? Second, many words have more than one definition. Would a player be required to know them all, or just one? Third, some words are notoriously difficult to define. It is one thing to define TAPIOCA. It is quite another to define ENNUI, LOVE, BEAUTY, and INSOFAR. It is true that expert players often play words that they cannot adequately define. So? Do you know how your automobile engine works? Would you be willing to forgo using it until you find out? I am grateful that the proper beating of my heart does not depend upon my knowing how and why it beats.

2

How to Play the Game

Many years ago I played on a city league slow-pitch softball team in Binghamton, New York. Our team made it to the playoff finals in its first year of existence and won the league championship the following two seasons. Despite our outstanding record, we looked like losers. The other teams had uniforms, about fifteen bats each, and bulging muscles. We were a bunch of ragtags who had no uniforms and three bats to choose from. For the first few games we were intimidated by the opposing team's batting practice. A succession of Neanderthals would step up to the plate, take hefty swings, and smite balls into the stratosphere.

We were able to win because softball, like all great games and sports, allows mind over matter to prevail. *Mind* in this sense means knowing how to play. We noticed, for example, that most of the ball fields we played on had no fences. Our outfielders would simply retreat when confronted with a heavy hitter, resulting in many long fly outs. In contrast, we practiced hitting line drives and ground balls. This type of contact was most likely to get us on base, either through base hits or from opponents' errors. We also practiced fundamentals such as hitting the cutoff man, backing up throws from the outfield, tag plays, and the like. We played an intelligent game.

In SCRABBLE, the player who is a "walking dictionary" is the counterpart of softball's Goliath. It cannot be denied that word knowledge is of great importance in SCRABBLE, just as it cannot be denied that physical strength can be used to advantage in softball. However, of even greater importance is knowing how to play the game, and that is what this book is all about.

CHAPTER 4

Scoring Points

This chapter is concerned with the ability to find high-scoring plays. It is not about longer-term strategic considerations. A well-developed scoring ability is necessary for sound strategic play, however. Imagine, for example, that you are ahead by 40 points late in the game and you wish to close down the board to protect your lead. This is a strategic consideration. You will not be able to accomplish this if you are unable to assess accurately which openings on the board are the most dangerous ones.

The key to maximizing your score is to look for locations on the board that harmonize well with the tiles on your rack. The expert player does not examine every possible play. Her attention is instead drawn to those portions of the board that are most relevant to the situation. One must be aware of both the available premium squares and the hidden possibilities implicit in the board position. I shall use the following diagram to illustrate these ideas.

Simple openings

A simple opening is one that allows a play to be made from, through, or to a letter of one previously played word. Only one word is added to the game board.

There are several places on this board where simple openings may be utilized for high-scoring plays. The most obvious one is column A. With the Q placed on A13, possible plays range from QUA for 36 points to words such as ROQUE, TOQUE, SILIQUE, SILIQUA, ANTIQUE, MANQUE, BARQUE, BEZIQUE, CAZIQUE, and dozens of others. Less likely but also possible are triple-triple plays that score hundreds of points. POSTIQUE and PRATIQUE (A8) are two examples.

Other potentially high-scoring simple openings are those permitting combination premium square plays. These include B10 to B14 or B15 (a triple letter-double word combination), L1 to L4, L5, L6, or L7 (a double letter-double word combination), and the double-double word opening through the M at 5J (5E to 5K). The opening at B10 downward is particularly dangerous, as the Z has not yet played. Possible plays here scoring 68 points or more are ZANANA, ZENANA, ZETAS, ZIRAM, ZOEAE, ZOEAL, ZOEAS, ZONAL, ZONARY, ZONATE, ZOUAVE, and ZYMASE. The Z may also be played at L1 for 40+ points (there are numerous ZOO- words in the OSPD).

Hooks

A hook is a letter that can be added to the beginning or end of a word already on the board, transforming that word into a different one. The main word played is perpendicular to the hooked word. An obvious hook location on this board is at J1. A player holding the remaining C could convert HARMERS to CHARMERS and likely play along row 1 so that the horizontal word made would cover one of the triple word squares at H1 or O1.

Another hook location is at L15. PLOTTY is an adjective as well as a noun, and thus a word played down column L and ending in T at L15, forming PLOTTIEST, is a possibility.

Sometimes hooks are overlooked because the hook letter radically changes the new word's pronunciation (for example, SLANDER-ISLANDER, ALLIANCE-DALLIANCE, etc). Many hook plays elude even expert players. In a game played in the 1980 North American Championship, my opponent played MARQUES, 7H. He deliberated before making this move and momentarily could not decide whether to make the blank a B or an M (both BARQUES and MARQUES are OSPD-acceptable words). He made the wrong choice: I was able to make a big play down column O by using my S, converting MARQUES to MARQUESS. I ultimately won the game by 16 points, and the victory was due to my opponent's oversight.

Overlaps

An overlap is a multiple hook play. The main word played creates subsidiary words by hooking onto letters from a previously played word that is parallel and adjacent to the main play. These subsidiary words are usually adjacent to each other. Let's have another look at the previous board position:

An example of an overlap might be LOAVES, 14I. This play produces three two-letter words (LI, OE, and AS). Potentially high-scoring overlap locations are from 14I or 14J to or beyond 14N; and from N1 or N2 to N6. You should also be aware of premium squares that are adjacent to vowels or to medium- and high-point letters (2N, 4L, 5K, 6N, and 14J, for example). These openings permit two-way plays that are often worth 25 points or more. Typical such plays on this board might be GEY, K3; BAM, 2L; or YORE, 4L. The spot at H12 for a Y should be kept in mind as well.

Openings and hooks for bingos

The hook locations at 1J and L15 are of especial importance, as they are possible locations for seven-letter bingos. The other openings for seven-letter bingos are at N9–N15, where the bonus play must begin with two vowels (e.g., EARNERS, AUTUMNS, etc.), and 14I–14O, where the beginning three letters must be a consonant and two vowels (BAITERS), two consonants and a vowel (TRAILER), or an A or an O, a consonant, and a vowel (ABATERS, ORANGES).

It is important to keep in mind locations for eight- and nine-letter bingos. Strong players play about twice as many eight-letter as seven-letter bingos. There are many spots for eight-letter plays on this board. In addition to column A, eight-letter bingos may be played through the M or E in HARMERS, and the O or N in WAGONED. It is less likely that a bingo will be played through the R at 4J, though it is certainly possible to end a bingo here or with the R at F8. Nine-letter bingos are much rarer, but should be kept in mind when the board situation warrants it. RE at 11F-G suggests possible RE- prefix plays.

Inside plays

Inside plays occur when the main word played forms other words by filling in a space between tiles already on the board. Inside plays are thus special forms of overlaps. One example is the vertical play of AXIAL at E8, which creates three new horizontal words: TIDE (10D), TARE (11D), and ELAN (12D). Plays like this one require creativity and good board vision. I find many of them delightful, even aesthetically pleasing.

Word extensions

A word extension is a play in which a word already on the board is changed by adding letters before, after, or both before and after it. The play cited just above—AXIAL—is a word extension as well as being an inside play: -IAL is added to AX. It is also possible to add letters before AX only (e.g., RELAX, POLEAX, OVERTAX, TOADFLAX), or to add letters both before and after AX (ATAXIA, TRIAXIAL).

The most common word extensions are made by tacking on -S plurals, prefixes, and suffixes to previously played words. For example, if a player begins a game by plunking down RALLY (8H), his opponent might add -ING to the word for an easy 36 points. Other common prefixes and suffixes that can be used to extend words are BE-, UN-, DE-, NON-, OUT-, OVER-, SEMI-, -ERS, -IER, -EST, and -IEST.

Word extensions can be surprising. I once began a tournament game with HIVES, 8D. Late in the game, my opponent hooked a C onto it, creating CHIVES (8C) by making a vertical play down the C column. I was able to win the game on my last turn by extending CHIVES to ARCHIVES, 8A, for 48 points. And in another game, my opponent opened with MAKE, 8G. I had AAEBSTW in my rack. I extended MAKE to

MAKEBATES, which scored 54 points. On the board diagram above, if you had an S and an I on your rack you might consider transforming DELIGHTS to SIDELIGHTS (O1, 45).

Some experts enjoy learning long word extensions. The possibilities for playing them don't occur very often. When they do, however, they can lead to a challenge as well as to a high-scoring play. Imagine the shock on your opponent's face after you transform ROTATED to AUTOROTATED, DANCING to ROPEDANCING, or ORGAN to ORGANOLEPTIC. One of my dream plays is to modify UNIQUE by adding four letters in front of it that completely change the pronunciation of the UNIQUE portion of the word.[3]

Scoring records and norms

I often get asked the following three questions:

1. What is the greatest number of points you have ever scored on a single turn?
2. What is the greatest number of points you have ever scored in one game?
3. How many points do you average per tournament game?

The answers to these questions are (1) 266 (the play was AQUIFERS, and it covered two triple word scores), (2) 715, and (3) around 425. My high move and high game scores are not particularly distinguished in comparison with current North American records. High scores are freak events and do not reflect true playing ability, however. Only the third question gives you some idea of my playing strength, and it does that because I have specified to a limited extent the quality of my competition. One need not get hung up over numbers. While it is true that I have played well in most of the games in which I have scored 500 or more points, the scores in some of my most thoughtful wins have been in the 300–340 range. A 500+ score might mean that you played well. It could also mean that you were lucky, that your opponent was overmatched, or both.

---

[3] COMM-, forming COMMUNIQUE.

It cannot be denied, however, that if you play regularly in a sanctioned club and your average has been rising steadily, your play has been improving. SCRABBLE clubs vary greatly in strength. An average of over 300 in most clubs is respectable. A 350 average is above the mean, and an average of 400 is exceptional. Regardless of averages, you will never know how good you really are until you play against experts.

Incidentally, the North American record for the greatest number of points garnered on one turn in sanctioned club or tournament play is 365, and it was set by Michael Cresta of Massachusetts. The word was QUIXOTRY. The North American record for the greatest number of points scored by one player in a sanctioned SCRABBLE tournament game is 770, and that record was set by Mark Landsberg. Michael Cresta scored 830 points in his QUIXOTRY game, which was played in a SCRABBLE club.

CHAPTER 5

Strategy

The strategic element is what elevates SCRABBLE from an excellent game to an exquisite one. Unfortunately, strategy is also the most obscure and neglected part of the game. Casual players are unaware of the profundity and subtlety of thought that can underlie a great player's finest plays. Newspaper reporters and interviewers certainly are in the dark in this respect. They want to know about unusual words played, favorite words, highest-scoring plays, and so forth. Never has an interviewer asked me to explain the strategy behind what I thought was my best play in a game or in a tournament. A mastery of strategy is essential to winning consistently at the club or tournament level. We shall see that attainment of this mastery is no simple matter.

Before beginning, it is important to understand that strategic principles in SCRABBLE often interact with each other. It is frequently impossible to make a play in which all the game's principles are adhered to. Strategic ideas sometimes conflict with each other, and the proper assessment of which of these ideas should prevail can be very difficult, and in some cases is unknowable. The need to maximize scoring often conflicts with rack management, for example. The idea of conservation of resources will at times be diametrically opposed to the principle of playing away as many tiles as possible when tiles remaining in the bag favor doing so. Issues such as these are considered to some degree in this chapter and are more fully dealt with in the games section of this book.

For those of you who hate numbers I ask your forbearance for the next few pages, as I deal with simulation and leave valuation. Computer simulation is often used by SCRABBLE experts to justify which of several plays is best, and an explanation of it is necessary now, before we proceed deeper into the strategy jungle. Valuation is a key concept, as it gives us an idea concerning when we should sacrifice points in order to retain good tiles. As you shall see, however, math takes us only so far in SCRABBLE. Board positions in SCRABBLE are curious things. They can muck up the math so easily, because there is so much more to consider.

Uses and limitations of simulation

You go first, and your first rack is BDEELOS. What is the best play you can make? Ask two strong players and you might get two different answers. One might suggest LOBED (8H, 20), and the other might advocate BODE (8G, 14). People can get into serious arguments concerning such things. Without an objective way to resolve the issue, there is no way of knowing who is right. Or rather, let me be less definite: there should be a way to strive toward an unbiased objective answer, regardless of whether it is achievable.

One solution might be to sample the bag: play the competing moves over and over again on two different boards and evaluate the consequences after the opponent's best play response and one's own next play. This is called simulation. Needless to say, the simulation of moves by hand, hundreds or thousands of times over, is not practical.

Fortunately, two SCRABBLE-playing computer programs simulate (sim) SCRABBLE positions. One of them, Brian Sheppard's Maven, is no longer available. I mention it because it was very good, and because it is historically important in the development of SCRABBLE theory. The other program is Quackle. Quackle was developed by two SCRABBLE experts, Jason Katz-Brown and John O'Laughlin. It is available online.

Throughout this book I will occasionally report simulation results from Quackle in order to support reasoning in favor of one play or another, and the numbers I will be giving refer to a move's *valuation*. Valuation is defined by Jason Katz-Brown as *score + rack value before simulation, and (our scores – their scores + our rack value – their rack value) averaged over all the simulation iterations.* Without going into too much detail, what this all means is that a number can be assigned to each of several possible candidate moves on a given turn. The move with the highest valuation is the best play—but not all the time. If valuations for two moves are within ½ point of each other they are equally good, for practical purposes. Valuation differences ranging from ½ point to 3 points indicate a small but real superiority for the higher-valued word, and differences of greater than 3 points signify major differences between moves. With regard to the BDEELOS rack, after 3,000 iterations BODE had the higher valuation: 32.7 as compared to 31.3 for LOBED. Why is LOBED the weaker play? Let's save that for a little later (incidentally, neither play is the best play). For now, let us see how we can use numbers to predict simulation results— often accurately, but sometimes not.

Scoring versus leave

We will cover many strategic aspects of SCRABBLE, but surely the most important general principle underlying this game is that good play is based on the accurate application of probability theory. The best player in the world is the one who is better than anyone else at maximizing his winning chances on each move that he makes. There are many aspects to consider, such as board position, defense, game score, opponent strength, and so on. But for the moment let us assume the unassumable, embodied in the following ubiquitous phrase: *everything else being equal.* . . . This gives us a starting point. It allows us to begin assessing the goodness of competing plays without even looking at the board.

The correct determination for when to conserve good tiles in a leave versus when to play them away for greater scores is not easy. It's nice to be able to keep the good tiles, but not at the expense of sacrificing too many points. Some players are too miserly. They refuse to part with their S's when it is advantageous to do so, and they stubbornly cling to their blanks until they find a playable bingo. Other players, particularly beginners or kitchen table players, gleefully part with the blank for an extra point or two. Many years ago, a player in a tournament exchanged the blank. He tossed it back into the bag figuring "what the heck, it isn't worth anything."

What follows are some general guidelines for determining whether to spend or save. These guidelines will not automatically lead to clear, unequivocal choices for all your moves. You can, in fact, expect an average of about four borderline decisions per game. In order to keep your hair from turning gray prematurely, I would advise you to heed *Wapnick's Rule* in these situations:

Wapnick's Rule: When in doubt, take the additional points.

There is no particular truth to this rule. But it does save time.

The key idea presented here[4] is that the strength of a play can be assigned a numerical value based on the following simple formula:

valuation = score + leave

Leave, or rack leave, refers to the tiles left on the rack after making a play. Calculating the score of a play is easy, but where do we go in order to evaluate the leave? Fortunately, this has been already been done for us. Here are the values that Quackle uses for one-tile leaves:

□	A	B	C	D	E	F	G	H	I	J	K	L	M
25.6	−0.6	−2.0	0.9	0.5	0.3	−2.2	−2.9	1.1	−2.1	−1.5	−0.5	−0.2	0.6
N	O	P	Q	R	S	T	U	V	W	X	Y	Z	
0.2	−2.5	−0.5	−6.8	1.1	8.0	−0.1	−5.1	−5.5	−3.8	3.3	−0.6	5.1	

This table assumes that all the tiles in a SCRABBLE set are neutral—that the summed valuation of all one hundred of them is zero. Because the blank (represented in the table by the blank square) and the four S's are so positive, most of the remaining letters must therefore be negative to balance them out.

Do you need to memorize these numbers in order to play good SCRABBLE? To a certain degree I would say yes. It is good to know, for example, that usually you are wasting a blank if you play it for less than 26 points more

---

[4] Nick Ballard, Charlie Carroll, and Brian Sheppard presented it first, about twenty years ago, and at around the same time both Steve Gordon and Jim Homan came up with similar approaches. I am deeply indebted to them for much of this discussion, and to Jason Katz-Brown and John O'Laughlin for their work on generating the leave values that are used in Quackle.

How to Play SCRABBLE Like a Champion

than the next best play that keeps it on the rack. It is also worth knowing that in general an S is worth about 8 points, and that the Z, X, and Q are worth about 5, 3, and –7 points, respectively.

If you don't want to memorize all 27 values, try memorizing values for the blank, S, Z, X, and Q. You can approximate the rest. Categorize the remaining 22 letters into three groups: fair, mediocre, and poor. Valuations of the fair tiles hover around zero and include A, C, D, E, H, K, L, M, N, P, R, T, and Y. Mediocre tiles valuations congregate around –2 (B, F, G, I, J, O), and poor tiles are all close to –5 (U, V, W). Assign 0 to each of the fair tiles, –2 to the mediocre tiles, and –5 to the bad ones. It's easy to remember which letters belong in each category. All you need is a mnemonic for the mediocre tiles: FIGJOB. You won't forget about UVW, and by elimination you can approximate the values of the other tiles to zero.

Let us return to the opening rack of BDEELOS and apply our understanding of score plus leave valuation to it. The valuation of LOBED is:

$$20 \text{ (points scored)} + 8.3 \text{ (valuation of } E + S) = 28.3$$

For BODE we have:

$$14 \text{ (points scored)} + 8.1 \text{ (valuation of } E + L + S) = 22.1$$

LOBED seems to be the clear choice. However, we have already seen that BODE simulates higher than LOBED. How can this be?

Just as two poisons, sodium and chlorine, combine under certain circumstances to form a harmless substance known as salt, SCRABBLE tiles often combine with each other to produce a valuation that is markedly different from the sum of the two tiles. This happens because no tile is an island. Certain tile combos are more popular in the OSPD than other combos. In the SCRABBLE world, this is called synergy. For example, the Q is valued at –6.8. The U is worth –5.1. A leave of QU, however, is different from Q plus U. Its valuation is +1.2, not –11.9.

The Quackle guys have gone way beyond assigning a numerical value to each letter of the alphabet. They have assigned numbers to *every* one of the over 900,000 possible 1- to 6-tile leaves. ACDFH is valued at –3.27, IIUVWW checks in at –34.8, and so forth. Quackle thus applies brute force to account for synergy. Expert players instead must use judgment, as it would be impossible as well as idiotic to memorize all those numbers. An expert needs to have a good sense regarding what letters in the English language go well with which other letters. Nevertheless, a few guidelines might be helpful. Keep in mind, however, that there will always be exceptions.

Let's return to the opening rack of BDEELOS to observe a most important type of synergy—the addition of low-point tiles to a low-point leave. With regard to our comparison of the moves LOBED and BODE, there are certain positional aspects of LOBED that put it at a disadvantage compared to BODE (placement of a vowel between the double letter scores, putting an E between two double word scores, and exposing an extra letter for the opponent to play through). Nevertheless the main reason BODE outshines LOBED is that the valuation of its leave—ELS—is more than the sum of the three letters in it. It is 13.7, not 8.1. The valuation of LOBED's leave, ES, is 10.4—3.3 points less that the valuation of ELS, BODE's leave. This accounts for over half the 6-point difference in score, and the positional disadvantages of LOBED take care of the rest and more.

ELS is a stronger leave than ES because it adds a low-point tile to the mix. By doing so it increases the chances of drawing to a bingo. Watch what happens to valuations if we continue adding good low-point tiles to the leave.

S	8.0
ES	10.4
ELS	13.7
EILS	15.0
EILRS	22.9
AEILRS	28.7

We see that (1) adding an I to ELS increases the value of the leave, even though the I by itself has a valuation of –2.1; (2) tacking an R to an EILS leave raises its valuation by almost 8 points even though the R by itself is worth only 1.1 points; and (3) adding an A to EILRS raises the valuation of the leave by about 6 points even though the A is a slightly negatively valued tile by itself. (Caveat: this often does not work when adding I, O, or U to the leave.)

Armed with this information, we return to the BDEELOS opening rack problem one last time in order to come up with the play that is truly best. The six-letter leave of BDELOS is valued at a high 23.6, and the best play is therefore to exchange one E. We don't have to know the specific valuation number, but we do need to know that BDELOS forms bingos with four vowels accounting for thirty-three of the hundred tiles (ALBEDOS, BOLIDES, BOODLES, and BLOUSED/DOUBLES), as well as with a nice selection of consonants (BEHOLDS, BLONDES, BLOWSED, BOBSLED, BOLDEST, and BORDELS) accounting for another twenty-four. From this information we deduce that BDELOS must be a great leave.

The most important conclusion we can derive from the above discussion is that we need a set of guidelines for determining (1) the conditions under which the valuation of a leave can be approximated by adding up the valuations of the individual tiles in it, and (2) the conditions under which a leave's valuation is synergic—that is, it differs markedly from the sum of the individual tile valuations comprising it.

Nine valuation guidelines

Let's begin with the specific guideline that we can derive from the BODE versus LOBED discussion. It's the probably the most important one:

1. *Valuations of great five- and six-letter leaves (e.g., AENST, AERST, EINST, EIRST, AGINST; the well known TISANE, RETINA, and SATIRE stems, etc.) are very high, much higher than valuations of the individual tiles within them.* In many cases, a best play will be one in which a great five- or six-letter leave remains on the rack. Note that all of these leaves include an S.

Many such leaves are worth 27–35 points. The best is INSERT. It is valued at 35.4, or about half a bingo. If you have EINRSTY on your rack and you have the choice between playing SENTRY for 39 or dishing the Y somewhere for 13, fish[5] off the Y—assuming that the board isn't totally closed down for a bingo play on the next turn.

---

[5] In the olden days (before 1990 or so), a weak player was often described as a fish, and fishing was the term used to describe playing off a few letters for few points in the hope of playing a bingo afterward. Fishes back then *were* weak players, because they overfished, and they overfished because they couldn't find the best plays on the board. Nowadays it is understood that fishing makes the most sense when discarding one or two tiles, and when the leave is great. Letter combos such as AERT, ING, ERS, and IEST are better than random leaves, but normally they are not good enough to justify sacrificing lots of points.

	A	B	C	D	E	F	G	H	I	J	K	L	M	N	O
1	J	O	S	H				■							■
2		F	O	I	N				■						
3				V											
4			P	E	S										
5			U		A										
6		E	R	R	I	N	G			■			■		
7			R		L										
8	■			P	A	C	E	D							■
9					B		F	O	H						
10			■		L			T	A	V			■		
11				D	E										
12			M	E											
13		B	O	Y											
14		O	R			■									
15	W	A	N	T	E	D	■								■

You: 195 | Opponent: 198

Your rack: A E I R S T U

Opponent's last play: B O A (B13 22)

This example demonstrates one of the most extreme cases of appropriate point sacrifice that I know of. The rack of course translates to SATIRE plus U, and as the SATIRE stem is so outstanding[6] but the U by itself so poor, the logical play is to exchange the U. However, there is a 46-point play alternative: RESPACED, 8A. It turns out that although the valuations of exchanging the U and playing RESPACED are within a point of each other, the U exchange simulates a full 5 points higher than RESPACED. Why? There are three reasons: the AITU leave after playing RESPACED may be worse on this board than usual, as there are very few places to play such letters and score decently; the board cannot be shut down to prevent us from playing a bingo; and in the event that a bingo is not playable on our next turn (something that happens 24 percent of the time), RESPACED remains an option.

It makes sense to fish when the probability of playing a bingo on the next turn is extremely high, when the cost of fishing is low relative to other plays

---

[6] SATIRE combines with 18 of the 26 different letters in the alphabet to form seven-letter words. These 18 letters account for approximately 75 percent of the tile pool.

(e.g., scoring 20 versus 22 points) or when a prospective bingo is absolutely essential for winning the game. Given that there are multiple bingo lines available, exchanging the U is worth the point sacrifice. If the opponent makes a downward play from K10 in an attempt to block both openings, there is a good probability of forming an eight-letter bingo through one of the letters in his word.

Rack: A D G I N R S

In this situation, the obvious candidate plays are PARING (1E, 27) and SPADING (1D, 36). The best play, however, is PIPETTED (E1, only 13 points). The value of its leave, AGINRS, is a hefty 31.8 points! And indeed, in the simulation it runs a gigantic 10 points higher than SPADING and 13 points higher than PARING.

How can we figure out that AGINRS is such a good leave? We might intuitively know that these letters go together well. Or we might surmise that as AGINRS contains ING and three other good letters, it must be a terrific leave. Or we might be able to quickly determine that AGINRS combines with the vowels A, E, I, O, and a slew of consonants—B, C, D, G, H, M, N, P, T, V, and Y—to form bingos.

2. *The valuation of a good two-tile leave in which one of the tiles is an S (RS, SS, ES, HS, etc.) is worth about 10 points.* Good two-tile non-S combinations using the X or Z (XZ, EZ, YZ) top out at around 7 points. The best non-S low-point two-tile leave, ER, is worth only about 4 points. Two-tile leaves consisting of two low-point consonants (LN, LR, RT, etc.) are worth a point or two more than their additive valuations.

3. *The valuations for many two-tile leaves can be accurately estimated by adding up the valuations of individual letters, if the leave contains one vowel and one consonant, or if, in the case of a two-consonant leave, only one of the letters is worth 3 points or more.* Here is a sampling of some representative leaves:

Leave	Additive valuation	Quackle's valuation
One vowel, one consonant		
AC	0.3	1.5
AD	−0.1	0.1
AF	−2.8	−3.3
AG	−3.5	−3.1
AH	0.5	0.8
Two consonants, one worth less than 3 points		
CD	1.4	1.6
CL	0.7	2.3
CR	2.0	3.7
FL	−2.0	−0.3
MT	0.5	0.0

On the other hand, the true valuations of two-vowel two-tile leaves, and of leaves consisting of two high-point consonants, are considerably lower than the summed valuations of the two letters. Let's have a look at two-vowel leaves first.

The table on the next page shows Quackle's valuations for the two-tile, all-vowel leaves. As you can see, these are never good. If one of the vowels is an E, things aren't so bad, but if neither is an E, at least 7 points must be shaved off from the play's score in order to arrive at its valuation:

Leave	Quackle's valuation
Two vowels	
AA	−8.4
AE	−4.1
AI	−6.9
AO	−8.0
AU	−11.5
EE	−5.4
EI	−5.7
EO	−6.3
EU	−10.0
II	−11.7
IO	−9.2
IU	−14.5
OO	−11.3
OU	−13.3
UU	−18.8

The best three-vowel leave, AEI, clocks in at −9.0, and the worst, UUU, registers a hefty −29.0. Four-vowel leaves? The best of them, AEEI, has a valuation of −16.0. That is 14 points worse than its additive valuation of −2.1.

Things are less dire when the leave contains at least one consonant. In fact, everything depends on the specific tiles. AEIRT has one more vowel than consonant and exhibits positive synergy. Its valuation is 11.3, as compared to an additive valuation of −1.4.

4. *Valuations of all-vowel leaves are always lower than their additive valuations.* Subtract approximately:

    a. 4 points from the sum of their individual valuations for a two-tile leave.

    b. 7 points for a three-tile leave.

    c. 14 points for a four-tile all-vowel leave. Don't even think about making plays that result in five- and six-tile all-vowel leaves!

    d. All-vowel combos that include one or more O's or U's fare even worse when compared to their additive valuations.

Take care not to overload your leave with vowels or with consonants. If you keep five or more vowels or six or more consonants in the leave, the number of words that you could play on your next turn is likely to be much smaller than if the rack were more evenly balanced.

Despite the fact that there are more consonants than vowels in the tile distribution (56 to 42, counting the two Y's as consonants), too many vowels on the rack (vowelitis) is a more common affliction than too many consonants. There are a number of reasons for this. First, many consonants combine with each other in groups of twos and threes both at the beginnings of words (BL, BR, CH, CHR, CL, CR, DR, FL, FR, GL, GR, KN, PH, PL, PR, SC, SCH, SCR, SHR, SK, SL, SM, SN, SP, SPL, SPR, ST, STR, SW, TH, THR, TR, TW, WR) and at their ends (CK, FT, LM, LT, MB, MP, NT, SH, SK, SP, ST, TCH, PHY, GHT). As a result, it will often take only one available free vowel on the board or from the rack to make a play utilizing three or more consonants. Vowels do not go together quite as well. Although it is possible to rid oneself of a number of vowels if the right consonant is available (e.g., AGIO, EIDE, UNAI, UNAU, AREAE, AUREI, COOEE, OIDIA, URAEI), there are relatively few words serving this function as compared to the number of words that can be formed from many consonants and one vowel.

Second, all vowels are worth 1 point. A play made in order to dump vowels from the rack is therefore not likely to score well. In contrast, twenty-three of the consonant tiles are worth 3 points or more. Disposing of consonants is thus generally more profitable as well as easier than disposing of vowels. Finally, it is easier to play away more consonants than vowels when the rack is balanced. As a result, racks that are initially balanced may become vowel-heavy over three or four successive turns.

It is good policy to play for a leave that alleviates or guards against vowelitis. Consider the opening rack of AEIJORU. RIOJA (8D) scores 4 more points than JIAO (8G), but it is the weaker play. JIAO retains a consonant (the R to go with EU), whereas RIOJA does not. The ERU leave after playing JIAO is valued at –3.2, but the valuation of EU left on the rack after playing RIOJA is –10.0. RIOJA would have to outscore JIAO by 7 points for it to be as good as play as JIAO.

5. *The more high-point consonants in the leave, the worse the true valuation is compared to the leave's additive valuation.* Here are some examples of all-high-point consonant leaves:

Leave	Additive valuation	Quackle's valuation
Two consonants, each worth more than 3 points		
BC	−1.1	−2.3
CF	−1.3	−2.4
KV	−6.0	−9.0
MP	0.1	−1.1
VX	−2.2	−4.4
BCF	−3.3	−9.7
HMP	1.2	−1.0
BCMP	−1.0	−12.6
BCMVW	−9.8	−25.3

The H behaves a little differently than other high-point consonants. Many high-point consonants combine with it without exhibiting negative synergy, and of course CH is a great combination. Its valuation is 5.4.

Imagine that your opening rack is CCFTUVW. You could play CUT for 10 points, but the leave of CFVW is highly unpromising (its Quackle valuation is –20.1). None of these letters form many words with each other, which means that it will require a minimum of three more turns before having a decent chance to play a bingo. My choice would be to exchange all tiles or to exchange all tiles except one C.

6. *The valuation of a good low-point four-tile leave in which one or two tiles are S's (ENRS, EHRS, ELRS, ELST, AERS, EIRS, ERSS, etc.) is between 15 and 20 points.* Replace the S with another good low-pointer (AERT, EIRT, EINT, etc.), and you get valuations ranging from 7 to 12 points.

7. *Duplicate tiles in a leave sometimes result in negative synergy.* Conventional SCRABBLE wisdom dictates that one should avoid leaving more than one tile of the same letter on the rack, if possible. The underlying idea is that letter duplication restricts one's options. Fewer words can be made from most racks having duplicate letters than from other racks. Also, there is some danger in leaving duplicates of any 1- or 2-point letter, as a third or fourth letter of the same type might be plucked from the bag. Two-of-a-kind may not be much of a liability, but three-or-more-of-a-kind can be crippling.

There are of course thousands of words in the OSPD that contain letter duplicates. It is therefore important to understand that some duplicates are worse than others. It is usually the case that the lower the valuation of a particular letter, the greater the difference in valuation between retaining one of them or two.

Only the blank and the S benefit from duplication (at +19.3 and +3.3, respectively). Valuations of all other duplicates are worse than their corresponding singlet valuations, and they range from 1.5 points worse (F) to 9.0 points worse (V). Nevertheless, we need not resort to explaining the lower valuations on the basis of duplication. Two bad tiles of *any* kind are worse than two good ones!

The avoidance of tile duplication is not a completely worthless principle, however. It should be heeded when the choice is between duplication versus no duplication, *if the tiles have approximately equal valuations as singlets*. Consider the L and the T. Their valuations differ by a tenth of a point (−0.2 and −0.1, respectively). Leaving two L's on the rack results in a valuation of −3.0, and leaving two T's yields an even worse valuation of −3.4. A leave of LT is worth +1.0 points, however, which means that everything else being equal, it makes sense to avoid keeping LL or TT duplication if you can keep LT instead. With an opening rack of CLLMOTT, MOLT or COLT (8G) would thus be a much better play than MOLL or MOTT.

An important factor in determining the degree to which duplicate letters may impede your play is the board position. If, for example, your leave contains two Y's but there are nice openings available for them, there is little problem. On the other hand, if you have a blank or an S and bingo-conducive tiles accompanying the Y's, you most likely will have to play at least one Y away first before playing the bingo. You might even have to play both Y's away on separate turns.

Another consideration is the contents of the bag. Imagine the following scenario: only a few points separate your score from your opponent's, the board is closed with few opportunities for big scores, and there are eight tiles in the bag. Under these conditions, the winner is often the player who plays out first, as by doing so she adds double the value of her opponent's tiles on the rack to her score. So, you consider two moves. Both use four letters from your rack. Neither move creates glaring openings that your opponent is likely to take advantage of. One play scores 6 points more than the other, but the higher-scoring play results in a leave that includes two R's. The lower-scoring play retains only one R, and just one R has been played so far. There are six R's in a set, which means that three are unaccounted for. You must decide whether to grab the additional 6 points and risk facing tripled or quadrupled R's on your next rack after drawing from the bag, or to sacrifice the points in an attempt to make your next rack more flexible. If you end up with a glut of R's you will have a very difficult time playing out first. On the other hand, the additional points from your higher-scoring play may make the difference between defeat and victory.

Now imagine the same scenario as the one just described, with a major difference: four R's are already on the board. The determination of the correct play in both cases depends, of course, upon the specifics of the board, score, and the tiles remaining in the bag. In most cases, however, the correct move when three R's remain unseen will be the lower-scoring play. With no R's unaccounted for, it is more likely that taking the additional points is correct.

8. *Leave values generally are highest when the letters comprising them are all low-pointers (other than leaves that include a blank, Z, or X).* I used to think that it was a good idea to have one or two high-point tiles among the seven tiles on my rack, rather than more or none of them. (A high-point tile is one that is worth 3 or more points.) Such a balance might allow me to score well on those occasions when bingos were not playable. Now, however, I feel that it is important to dispense with the high pointers quickly, and that it is especially important to get rid of the negatively valued high pointers (BFJVW) rather than the better ones (CHKMP). More than 80 percent of all bingos played in tournaments have no or only one high-point letter in them. In the beginning of the game, and when the board is wide open, it makes a lot of sense to get rid of high-pointers as fast as possible. You will play many more bingos if you do.

Consider this opening rack: ABHINOO. There are two main choices here: HOBO (8E or 8G, 18) and ABOON (8H, 16). HOBO outscores ABOON by 2 points, and its AIN leave is another 1.3 points higher than the HO leave after playing ABOON. It "should" be 3.3 points better than ABOON, but it actually simulates almost 6 points higher. Clearly it makes little sense to keep the H in the hope of playing it for a lot of points on the next turn. Much better would be to play it away now, because it is easier to draw tiles forming a bingo from AIN on the rack than it is with HO on the rack.

9. *There are certain two-letter combinations that are like oil and water. They have negative synergy, and they combine to form relatively few words. At least one of the two letters should be played away as soon as possible.* These combinations are: BF, BP, BV, BW, CV, CW, FH, FK, FP, FV, FW, GK, JQ, JX, JZ, KQ, KV, KZ, MW, PV, PZ, QV, QW, QX, QZ, UW, VX, VZ, and WZ. Among the vowels, A and O do not combine particularly well. Even worse are combinations such as AAO, AOO, and AAOO. The number of points that should be sacrificed in order to make a play divesting the rack of the above combinations, as opposed to making a higher-scoring play that does not break them up, is variable. It depends on the particular combination on the rack, the board and score, the other tiles in the rack, and the tiles remaining in the bag. Keeping these combinations is a much bigger negative than most people imagine.

Useful as the above guidelines are, it's time to move on to a consideration of factors that make them sometimes worthless. If you would like to investigate leave valuations more thoroughly, get a copy of Quackle (it is online and free), set up a game, and click on the *Generate choices* button. The valuation of the leave for any particular play can be approximated by comparing the play's score and the valuation given for it.

Things that muck up the math

Sometimes a leave is worth Quackle's valuation for it, and sometimes it differs wildly from it, due to a multitude of additional factors unique to the particular game being played. Let's examine some of them.

Spending or saving the S

Everything else being equal, an S is worth about 8 points. It should be spent if the play using it yields at least 8 to 10 points more than plays not using it. This is not an ironclad rule. For example, if you are behind near the end of the game and can win only by playing a bingo, it might be necessary to keep the S even if using it would result in garnering an additional 20 or 30 points. The S becomes more valuable if the three other S's in the set are all showing on the board, as you may be able to prepare high-scoring S-hook plays that your opponent can neither use nor block. In this case, 10 points may not be sufficient compensation for the S. Finally, you would be ill-advised to spend the S for only 8 to 10 points if you also have a blank on your rack but no playable bingo, and there are openings on the board for playing bingos. In this case, you should raise your threshold for spending the S to perhaps 12 to 15 points versus not playing it. The blank combines very well with an S for forming bingos, and the ☐ S valuation is 37.4, almost 4 points higher than the additive valuation for the tiles. You should not jeopardize the bingo opportunity by playing away the S without lots of compensation.

If you have two S's on the rack, you should freely spend one of them for a good deal less than the additional 8 or more points. Under most conditions, having two S's is only about 3 points better than having one S. The S duplicate has some value, but it is not a treasure.

In some instances, playing away an S for an additional three or four points will telegraph to your opponent that you are holding another S in your rack. Consider the opening rack of ACEFHSS. You would like to play CHAFES (8C, 36), but tacking the S onto CHAFE for 4 more points lets your opponent know that your remaining tile must be another S. Why else would you spend the S for so little? Having realized this, your opponent would be less likely to make a play that would give you an S-hook than if you had made a play that better disguised your rack leave. Simulation of CHAFES versus CHAFE (8D, 32) reveals that they are equally good. I would choose CHAFE, however, in order to deprive the opponent from knowing what is on my rack.

Let's now deal with a situation in which playing away two S's at the same time scores a few more points than playing away one or no S's.

Rack: A E I O S S

The highest-scoring play in which only one S is used is SAE (6H, 18). OASES (6F, 22) uses two of the three S's and scores 4 more points; OASIS (and the positionally worse OSSIA) at 13J score the same as SAE but have better leaves (IS and ES, versus IOSS). OASES and OASIS are the best moves. In fact, they are 5.4 and 5.0 points better than SAE, respectively, more even than the four additional actual points they score. Even though two S's are kept after SAE, the IOSS leave is not very promising, either for separate high-scoring S plays or for creating a bingo. The IS and ES leaves after OASES and OASIS are much superior. Incidentally, if you are unfortunate enough to have three or all four S's clogging up your rack, you might consider playing them away rather than exchanging them. That way, your opponent will not be able to pick them. But this isn't a big deal, as there is just under a 50 percent chance that you will pick any S that you throw back into the bag.

Spending or saving the blank

Given that the blank's valuation is 25.6, it makes sense to play it if it nets an additional 26 or so points as compared with other plays that do not spend it.[7] As was the case with the S, however, there often are extenuating circumstances. Consider the following: your opponent goes first and exchanges one tile. By doing so, she lets you know that she is very close to a bingo. You have CDHMPZ☐ on your rack. Your options are to exchange tiles (best is to keep CH☐), to play CHEZ (8F) or PHIZ for 34 points, or perhaps to play CHUMP (8D or 8H, 32). Had the opponent not exchanged one tile, keeping CH☐ and exchanging the rest would have been the best play. But PHIZ is correct now, because it is so good defensively. PHIZ allows no hooks, and your opponent may well be unable to play an eight-letter bingo through your letters.

Occasionally you will have two blanks on your rack and the opportunity to play away either one or both of them for big scores. The valuations of a one- and two-blank leave are 25.6 and 44.8, respectively. It therefore makes sense to choose the higher-scoring two-blank play if the points garnered from it exceed the lower-scoring one-blank play by 20 or more points.

It is extremely rare to find situations in which it is advantageous to play one blank when two are on the rack and the two can be played together for a bingo. One borderline case is shown here:

---

[7] Personally, under most circumstances I wouldn't play it unless I got at least 30 points for it. Getting 26 points just doesn't seem enough.

	A	B	C	D	E	F	G	H	I	J	K	L	M	N	O
1															
2															
3															
4															
5															
6						W									
7						H									
8					O	B	E	Y							
9					M										
10					P		C	A	N	N	I	E	S	T	
11		E	R	A	S	I	O	N							
12							V								
13						E									
14						R									
15						T									

You: 100 | Opponent: 196

Your rack: B I O S X ☐ ☐

Opponent's last play: CANNIEST (10H)

There are many playable bingos on this board, the best of which are ICEBOXES, BOLLIXES, SUBOXIDE (all for 98 points, the first two at 13B and the last at H1) and SUBOXIDE (M3, 96). There are also three plays that utilize only one of the two blanks: BOXIEST (O4, 54) and TOXINS or TOXICS (O10, 60).

The position is quite complex. Any of the bingos virtually ties the game, but at the cost of using both blanks plus allowing the opponent opportunities to play first on a very wide-open and dangerous board. TOXINS is not as weak defensively, but it keeps the B along with the blank, and this lowers the likelihood of playing a bingo next turn. BOXIEST scores the least, but offers good long-term prospects—the board is kept wide open for a bingo, which you are more likely than your opponent to play, but the triple word squares in column O are no longer available for your opponent. Simulation favors the three 98-point bingos by about 3 points over TOXINS or TOXICS, and by 6 points over BOXIEST. Nevertheless, the non-bingo plays probably offer the best chances for winning the game.

Conserving specific tiles other than the S and the blank

Depending on the board situation, any tile in the bag may be a great deal more valuable at a given moment than it normally is. If you are holding such a tile, you should save it if plays not using it score slightly less than or the same as plays requiring it to be spent.

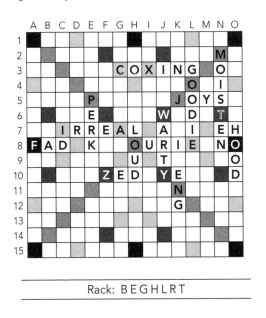

Rack: B E G H L R T

In this example, the best plays—GLOB and GLOBE at H1—dispense with the G and keep the H. BROTH (H1, 33) scores as well as GLOBE and better than GLOB, but it plays away the H. There are two good locations for the H: 6F and 2J. Given that holding on to the H guarantees a minimum score of 26 points next turn, it makes sense to retain it.

	A	B	C	D	E	F	G	H	I	J	K	L	M	N	O
1	T			Q	U	A	G	S							C
2	I			U											A
3	N		A	I											R
4	C		I	N											O
5	A	I	R												T
6	L	O													E
7		N										G			N
8	B	I	P	O	D		F	I	Z		O	R	A	T	E
9		U	H			K	A	F			D	E	X		
10		M	O	O	L	A						E			
11			N		S	T	E	E	V	E	D				
12	V	I	E	W			G					I			
13	A		D				R					E	H		
14	T						E					R	E		
15	U						T						Y		

Adam: 346		Dave: 349

Adam's rack: B I L O S W Y

Dave's last play: QUAGS (1D, 45)
Unseen tiles: A E J L M N O P R S ☐ ☐

This position is from a game played between former World, U.S., and Canadian champion Adam Logan, and 2005 and 2009 National Champion Dave Wiegand. It is Adam's turn and he played YOW (N2, 35). He should have conserved his Y, for had he picked either the M or the P out of the bag, MITY, PATY, or PITY (N6, 42) would have been possible next turn, assuming Dave didn't block it. This is why BOW at N2 simulates over 6 points higher than YOW.

The third and fourth U's with the Q unplayed and not on your rack

If you and your opponent are within 50 points of each other near the end of the game, getting stuck with an unplayable Q is likely to spell disaster. A player with a 50-point lead and a Q but no U on the rack has at best a 30-point lead, since the opponent will gain at least 20 points upon going out. In addition, the opponent often may be able to score many points by playing one tile away at a time, as there is no pressure to go out first. The recent OSPD additions of QAT, SUQ, TRANQ, and especially QI, which has become the most often played word in SCRABBLE, have made the Q a less frightening tile than it had been. Still, people get stuck with it sometimes.

If the Q has not been played but both blanks and two or three U's are on the board, and there are no openings for U-less Q words, keep one U on your rack unless its use is required for a very high-scoring play. This is especially true if the score is close and the game is nearing its conclusion. Remember that with six or fewer tiles in the bag you will not be able to exchange the Q.

Dealing with consonant glut

Having too many consonants on the rack is a particular concern when (1) the board is closed, so there are no useful vowels on it to play through; (2) the consonants do not work well with each other; and (3) there are few vowels left in the bag. Under any of these conditions, you must make a choice between exchanging tiles and making the best possible play, taking into consideration the totality of the game situation.

Here is an example in which the score, the nature of the board, and knowledge of the unseen tiles all help determine the best play:

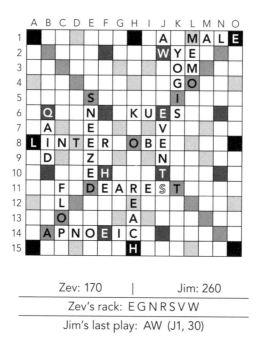

Zev: 170 | Jim: 260

Zev's rack: E G N R S V W

Jim's last play: AW (J1, 30)

This position is from a game played between two experts, Zev Kaufman and Jim Kramer. It is Zev's turn. He is down 90 points, and he has too many consonants. He needs a quick bingo to have a chance of winning the game, because he will have to play two of them to overtake Jim. He can exchange tiles in the hope of picking a bingo (best would be to hold on to ENRS and exchange the rest), or he might go for points by playing GNOME (3I, 26) or VENOMS (3H, 30). GNOME retains both the V and W—terrible for bingo making. And VENOMS sheds the S, leaving GRW. Not good.

Zev made the best play, which was VOW (E13, 9). He left himself with two chances to pick one of the fifteen unseen vowels, which would give him ANGERS, INGERS, or ONGERS, all great leaves, plus a tile. By getting rid of the V and W and keeping the E and S, he gave himself a good shot at a bingo.

Playing away many tiles?

In the early days of tournament SCRABBLE, it was widely believed that playing away many tiles was better than playing away few tiles. The rationale for this belief was as follows: If there are only a few really terrific tiles in a SCRABBLE set (the two blanks, the four S's, and the X and Z), then by playing longer words than your opponent, you increase the likelihood that you will pick more great tiles than he will. This in turn should increase the probability of you winning the game.

The flaw in this thinking is that playing away more letters also increases the probability of picking more U's, V's, and W's than the opponent. Furthermore, it doesn't take into consideration the quality of the leave. Imagine the extreme example of SATIREQ. No one would play SATIRE, even though it expends six whole tiles.

Picking extra tiles doesn't markedly improve one's chances of picking the great tiles anyway. Suppose you go first and you are trying to decide between a three- and a six-letter word. While it is true that you double your chances of picking a blank by playing away six tiles rather than by playing away three, in reality all you are doing is increasing the probability of picking at least one blank from seven percent to fourteen percent. This means that on one out of every thirteen draws, the extra three tiles played away will result in obtaining one extra blank. That isn't worth giving up even a couple of points.

Nevertheless, the idea of playing away as many tiles as possible is not totally without merit. There are times when it overrules almost every other consideration. Imagine, for example, that the score is close, there are seven or eight tiles in the bag, and among the unseen tiles is a blank. Whoever gets it will likely win the game, so it makes a lot of sense to play a longer word rather than a shorter one, even if the move's valuation isn't as high as that of a shorter word. Also—assuming that the tiles remaining in the bag are not unusually junky—if I had to choose between two plays that score about the same number of points, have approximately the same leave valuation, and do not differ markedly in what they offer the opponent, I would play the longer word. The leaves of F and GORTU are both worth –2.2 points. If there is good stuff unseen, I would rather play a six-letter word and keep the F than play a two-letter word and retain GORTU.

The real and imagined dangers of defense

Defense in SCRABBLE is necessary, even crucial at key moments, but in general it is overrated. Let me restate that: unless you have a pretty good idea from your opponent's previous move(s) that she can hurt you—that is, she seems to be hoarding good tiles and fishing off bad ones—it rarely pays to sacrifice either points or leave valuation in order to limit your opponent's possibilities. Sure, it is good strategy to deny your opponent access to premium squares and openings for playing bingos—but not if you have to give up much, or even some, in order to do it.

Defense makes sense if (1) you have a lead to protect, (2) your tiles aren't as good as you think your opponent's tiles are, (3) the bag is empty or close to it, (4) there is something unusual about the board (e.g., there is an S-pluralizable bingo ending just before a triple word score on it, or something else that is glaringly dangerous), and/or (5) it costs you very little in terms of score and leave. Remember that by limiting your opponent you may also be obstructing your own game. You should take care to block only those openings that your opponent is likely to utilize before you do. If you have a blank in your rack but no playable bingo, making a play that blocks a spot for your bingo on a subsequent turn is like shooting yourself in the foot.

Let's begin our discussion of defense by examining some opening racks. At this point, you know nothing about your opponent's rack. Defense is not a primary consideration, but that doesn't mean that it should be ignored completely.

Creating an S hook

Your rack consists of AAIILOV, and your two best plays are VIOLA and VOILA (8D, 24). VOILA doesn't take an S hook, so a comparison of how these plays simulate gives us an idea of how dangerous it might be to create an S hook at the beginning of the game. VOILA sims 1.1 points higher than VIOLA. Everything else being equal, make the play that doesn't hook an S, unless you keep an S in your leave.

Making a play that might be extended to a triple word score

Now let's investigate the dangers of plays an opponent might make by extending your opening play to a triple word score. Your opening rack is HHORTWW. There are seven moves that score 30 points each: ROWTH, THROW, WORTH, and WROTH at 8H, and WHORT, WORTH, and WROTH at 8D.

We should expect WROTH (8D) to come out best in the simulation. It doesn't take an S plural, and it can't be extended to a triple word score. Next best should be WROTH at 8H, which suffers ever so slightly in comparison to the 8D placement only in that it can be extended to WROTHFUL, a highly unlikely event. Next best might be WHORT (8D), WORTH (8D), and ROWTH (8H), all of which can be pluralized but not extended for big scores. Unlike the other plays, ROWTH places the vowel between two double letter scores. But because of the HW leave, it is unclear whether this is a deficiency or an advantage. My suspicion is that it is an advantage. On the other hand, ROWTH can be morphed into GROWTH and TROWTH—a very slight disadvantage with neither a G nor a T in the leave. All of the three remaining plays at 8H take S's and also can be extended: THROWERS, THROWING, WHORTLES, WORTHFUL, WORTHIER, WORTHIES, WORTHILY, WORTHING.

The simulation reveals WROTH (8H) to be best. Within a point of it, however, are all three 8D plays and ROWTH, 8H. THROW is 1½ points worse than WROTH, and WORTH is 2 points worse. These are not major differences. Nevertheless, every little bit helps.

Placing a vowel next to a double letter score

Now let's look at the danger of placing a vowel adjacent to a double letter score. If you decide to play a word such as BARMY or PORCH, should you play it at 8H for two more points than at 8D in order to avoid playing the vowel adjacent to double letter scores?

It turns out that, everything else being equal, exposing a vowel to the double letter scores is worth about ½ point to the opponent. It is thus almost always better to take the higher scoring play and expose the vowel to the double letter scores.

Consider the opening rack of DIGPUVY. PUDGY is the best play, but should it be made at 8D or 8H? Placement at 8H puts the vowel adjacent to the double letter squares at 7I and 9I. The opponent might be able to score well by making a parallel play using an M, P, or (heaven forbid) an X. However, it turns out that PUDGY at 8H sims 1.6 points higher than at 8D.

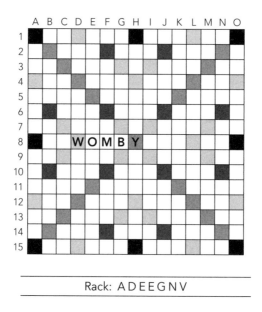

Rack: A D E E G N V

In this example, AVENGED is playable at 7H or 9H. The 7H placement is correct. If AVENGED is played at 9H and if your opponent has the X and a U, she will score 52 points on her next turn by playing XU at 10J. After the 7H placement, however, the opponent's X is considerably less dangerous. The likelihood is that your opponent will not have an X and a U in her rack, but why take chances? And indeed, AVENGED at 7H sims ½ point better than it does at 9H. Note that the difference between the two options is again so small that it wouldn't be worth it to play AVENGED at 7H if the play scored even 1 point less than at 9H.

Placing a high-point letter next to premium squares

Try to avoid making plays in which high-point tiles are placed next to double or triple word squares in such a manner that a vowel placed on the premium square forms a two-letter word with the high-point tile.

You can make quite a substantial error if you don't heed this advice, as in this example:

Rack: C E I O R R X

What we are interested in here is the comparison between EXCITOR and XEROTIC—both at K4, both scoring 32 points, and both retaining the same leave, an R. XEROTIC is defensively negligent because it places the X next to a double word square. A vertical play down column L and hooking an I or a U onto the X at L4 would score a lot of points. EXCITOR, on the other hand, has the E adjacent to the double word score. This isn't exactly defensive either, but it is much safer than having the X at K4. Simulation reveals a considerable 5-point edge for EXCITOR over XEROTIC.

Opening a triple word score

Non-expert players are often inordinately fearful of making a play that opens up access to a triple word square. Maybe this has to do with the deep redness of these squares. Red is the color of danger, so opening a triple word score must be dangerous, right? We will see that in the absence of compelling evidence that the opponent has great tiles, it makes little sense to sacrifice many points or quality of leave in order to avoid opening up a triple word score.

Rack: E E G I H N V

There are two ways of allowing access to a triple word square. The first is to make a play that can be hooked. HIVE (D11) is an example, as a D or an S can be tacked onto it at 15D. The second way is to make a play that puts a letter in a triple word square lane. The two highest simulating plays in this position do this. They are HIVE (D1, 32), and HIVES (4A, 30). There are other plausible options that don't open a triple word score (e.g., GIVE and GIVEN, 10H, and VEIN at J6). Let's examine the simulation results to get an idea of how dangerous HIVE (at D1) and HIVES actually are. HIVE sims about 2 points higher than HIVES, so let's compare that move with

GIVEN, which is slightly better than GIVE and which does not open a triple word score. Compared to HIVE, GIVEN scores 5 points less, and its EH leave is another 1½ points worse than HIVE's EGN leave. Everything else being equal, HIVE thus should simulate between 6 and 7 points higher than GIVEN. Everything else is of course not equal—there should be some downside to HIVE for opening up a triple word score row! And in fact there is a downside, because HIVE sims a little over 4 points better than GIVEN, not 6 to 7 points better. It appears that opening up the triple word score lane in this case incurs a penalty of about 2 points.

Generalizing from this specific example has its limits. Putting a Z in a triple word square lane is worse than putting the H in the same spot. Placing an S or an E at 1D in place of the H might raise the probability of the opponent playing a triple-triple. Moreover, the exact tile placement in the triple word score row is an important consideration. An open H at 1B (think words beginning with CH, SH, TH, and WH) may be a lot more dangerous than an open H at 1D. Nevertheless, I would be surprised if it ever makes sense to sacrifice more than 5 points in move valuation to avoid putting a letter in a triple word score lane.

The expert player does not play to avoid catastrophe. He instead plays the odds. In the situation above, he does not ruminate on disaster, e.g., "If I play HIVE or HIVES, my opponent might be able to crush me with WISHBONE." He makes the play that is most likely to result in winning the game. He knows that for a significant proportion of turns in situations like this, the opening he has created will not even be used. The opponent may not have good tiles or may have a better play elsewhere. The opponent may even feel obliged to block the opening if she cannot take advantage of it. Most of the time, however, the opening will be taken, usually for from 21 to 33 points. If the opponent has tiles good enough to score very well here, she likely would have been done almost equally well somewhere else on the board.

Of course there is *some* risk that an opponent might play a triple-triple bingo through a letter you place in a triple word score lane. Such a play will almost always score over 100 points. Nevertheless, the alternative strategy of *never* placing a letter in harm's way will lead to more losses over the long run than will taking the small risk of doing so. Sure, the player who adopts the strategy I am proposing will be hurt by the occasional big play. It's built into the system. Take a small risk many times over, and eventually you get burned.

One more thing about opening triple word score rows or columns: before doing so, be aware of the significance of your opponent's last play. In a recent game, my opponent played into a triple word row right after I exchanged one tile. Not smart, because my exchange indicated that I had excellent tiles remaining on my rack. I played a triple-triple bingo on my next turn. Also, it makes little sense to allow the opponent a chance at a triple-triple if you are winning by over 100 points. Why give him an opportunity to beat you?

One must be wary of creating triple word square openings that permit *likely* damaging counterplays. Such plays should be avoided. Here is an example:

Rack: A A D E E I Z

I would not play AZIDE (9H) here (there are better plays anyway). If my opponent had an H, M, P, W, or Y, he likely would score well over 40 points by making a simple horizontal four-letter word beginning at 8L.

How to Play SCRABBLE Like a Champion

I would also avoid opening a triple word square on a board that is otherwise bereft of scoring opportunities. In this case, the discrepancy between what the opponent might have scored had the opening not been created and what the opponent would be likely to score from using the new opening may more than offset the additional points.

Sometimes your opponent's play will create an opening for you that you cannot use. In this situation, you have three options: (1) block the opening so that your opponent cannot take advantage of it; (2) ignore the opening and play elsewhere; and (3) create a second opening. The idea behind creating a second opening is that after you have made your play and picked fresh tiles from the bag, there will be at least one opening on the board for you to take advantage of. The disadvantages of creating a second opening are that you may have to forgo a higher-scoring play elsewhere on the board in order to create the opening, and that your opponent gets his choice of two openings rather than access only to the one he created by his last move. Furthermore, the two openings are rarely equal in value, and your opponent gets the first shot at the better one. The strategy sometimes even backfires: your opponent takes one of the two openings, and you cannot use the other. I generally shy away from creating second openings unless the play is good for other reasons (e.g., it scores many points, balances the rack, and so forth).

Let the game score dictate strategy

It is not overstating the case to say that everything depends on the game score. A move that is ideal if you are 50 points behind your opponent may be disastrous if you hold a 50-point lead.

Block when you are ahead

Imagine that the game is coming to a close, you are up by 40 or 50 points—enough to survive anything but a bingo—and there are great tiles still in the bag or on your opponent's rack. You have to defend your lead by blocking bingo lanes.

This scenario is very common. Sometimes the task is easy, but at other times it requires some cleverness. Here is a situation in which making the right defensive move is critical, even though the player on the move is slightly behind rather than ahead:

	A	B	C	D	E	F	G	H	I	J	K	L	M	N	O
1								P			N				
2					W		R		K	I					
3	O			Q	I		O		E	N					
4	B			U	T		P	A	R	E					
5	L			O				E	F	S					
6	I			T				R							
7	G			H			G	O	L	D					
8	A		J	A	M	B	E	S							
9	T	H	I	O		E		T	A	V					
10	E					I			T	I					
11		U		U	N	D	Y		A						
12	E	N	U	F		I		E							
13		S	M	A	Z	E		G							
14	D	E						G							
15	O	W						S							

Dave: 294	Joe: 311

Dave's rack: A C E E N O T

Joe's last play: GOLD (7H, 10)

Unseen tiles: A A C D I I L L N O R R R V X Y ☐

This game was played between two very strong experts: Dave Wiegand, a two-time Nationals champion, and Joe Dackman, a strong West Coast player. Joe had just played GOLD, and the determination of Dave's best play must be considered with this in mind. GOLD opens the board for an S hook, and makes sense *only* if Joe has the blank on his rack. Dave thus should have played defensively. Instead he tried OCEAN (8K, 33), after which Joe played VIRIDIAN (N2, 70), locking up the win.

The correct play was found in post mortem analysis by Marlon Hill. It is CANOE (K10, 23). CANOE gives Dave a chance at winning, although not a great chance. He will be ahead by only 6 points, with Joe holding the blank. Nevertheless, CANOE makes it almost impossible for Joe to bingo on his next turn. In addition, Dave retains the last E, a valuable tile (this is why CENOTE, in the same place as CANOE, is a much worse play— it spends the E *and* empties the bag, double negatives that amplify rather than cancel each other out). Even though simulation shows OCEAN and

OCTAN far ahead of CANOE (K10, 23), Quackle's simulation brain didn't take into consideration the meaning of Joe's GOLD play.

You: 321 | Opponent: 307

Your rack: C I I O R S Y

Consonants from which two-letter words cannot be made (C and V) and from which two-letter words can be made with only one vowel (J, Q, Z) can be very useful for closing down the board. In this situation, the two blanks remain among the thirty-three unseen tiles. The correct strategy is to block the M and N columns—the only locations for bingos on this board—without creating any new openings, while at the same time scoring enough points to make winning likely if the opponent cannot play a bingo. Very effective in accomplishing all of this is SIC (N4, 28). Nothing can be hooked onto its C to make a vertical play. A play like COSY (N2, 35) scores more, but opens up column O. In this situation, why give your opponent *any* counterplay? With a 42-point lead and the possibility of YOD (12H, 30) on your next turn (don't play it now!), the win is likely.

	A	B	C	D	E	F	G	H	I	J	K	L	M	N	O
1						L							D		Z
2					H	E							A	R	E
3				B	O	T							W	A	E
4			Y	A	M	S								I	
5			O	N	E						P	R	A	N	K
6		Y	U	N										W	
7	Q	I		E			T	H	U	D			E		L
8	U	N		D	O	J	O					V		A	I
9	E					I	N	T	E	R	I	O	R	S	
10	E	F			V						C				
11	N	A	D	O	G	E					A				
12		C	R	O	P						R				
13	W	E													
14	I	T													
15	G														

You: 313 | Opponent: 291

Your rack: A I B F S T X

Opponent's last play: VICAR (L8, 28)
Unseen tiles: A E G I I L L M O S T U ☐

Don't get too greedy if you are ahead late in the game. The object is to win; point spread is a secondary consideration. Sometimes an "obvious" offensive move can jeopardize winning chances.

Here you should *not* play AX at either 6I or 10I. These plays score over 50 points each, but with an S and a blank unaccounted for, and considering that your opponent opened the board on his last play, you might as well block bingo openings while keeping AX in the leave. Use the S in your rack defensively to safeguard your victory: play SIFT (12G, 23). This play greatly reduces the probability of playing a bingo along row 13, which is the only available bingo lane, except for an unlikely GE- bingo at 15A.

Your future strategy should be clear. After SIFT, there are two tiles left in the bag. If your opponent opens a new bingo lane on his next turn (e.g., FA, I12), calculate whether he can beat you with his best possible bingo after you play AX (6I) to go up by 94. If he cannot, then go ahead and play AX. If he can (and that could be a possibility if you leave the right tiles in the bag after playing SIFT), then close down the bingo lane at all costs, even if you have to play away the X. If he plays elsewhere (a blunder, because such a play would essentially concede the game to you), make your big X play. If he blocks or uses the triple letter squares at both 6J and 10J (e.g., by making a play such as MULE, J6), play AX at H1. In a situation like this one, timing is crucial. Play defensively first to secure the win; score well afterward.

You: 368 | Opponent: 344

Your rack: E G G L N N S

Opponent's last play: QUINOA (D1, 50)
Unseen tiles: D D E E I I I L N R S T U U □

The previous three examples demonstrated how the board can be closed down to preserve a lead. Would that it were always so easy! It often happens that your opponent has more than one opening on the board where she can play a bingo or otherwise score well in order to overtake you.

In this case, only eight tiles remain in the bag, and a blank and an S are as yet unaccounted for. You should play defensively to maintain your lead, but how?

Note that there are *no* unseen high-point tiles. This means that the only way to lose this game is to allow your opponent to bingo. As the big tiles have all been played, you need not worry much about the non-bingo openings available such as column O and row 5. You in fact might be able to take advantage of these openings on subsequent turns to maintain your lead (e.g., with FENS, 1L, or NOGS, 5C).

The available bingo locations on this board are N4–10 (yes, WHEW is a noun and takes an S plural), along row 10 (beginning at 10G, 10H, or 10I), and 6A-H. The last opening is probably the least dangerous, due to its limited flexibility: an eight-letter bingo is required, and its fourth letter must be an A. Attention should therefore be focused on the other openings first. You are unable to use the S hooks at 10I and N6 to block both row 10 and column N. There is another way, however: GLOBE, M10! It scores only 8 points, but a 32-point lead with a decent rack leave and only six tiles left in the bag should make you feel pretty comfortable. Unless your opponent opens up a new bingo alley next turn, you should block the 6A opening on your next play, probably with NOGS. The idea is that if you cannot block your opponent completely, at least block his most likely bingo line. Your opponent must bingo next turn, open a new bingo alley (not so easy on this board), or lose.

In situations in which you have a lead and the board is completely wide open, you should take the offensive. Play to maintain your lead by scoring a lot of points rather than by trying to limit your opponent. Defending an open board against a good player is an almost hopeless task.

Open up the board when trailing

If you are losing, strive for an open board with numerous scoring chances. The only way to catch up is to outscore your opponent, and if the board is closed so that no bingos can be played and few high-scoring non-bingo opportunities are available, chances are great that you will lose. Create an opening. If there is a bingo line open but you can't use it immediately, open another line somewhere else far away. You may get slaughtered, but you will at least have some hope of winning. Always give yourself a chance to win.

Most plays that open the board are rather straightforward. Here is one from a 2008 Can-Am Challenge game, played by yours truly and David Koenig:

	A	B	C	D	E	F	G	H	I	J	K	L	M	N	O
1															
2															B
3															R
4						C	O	N	F	E	R	V	A
5								H							C
6						G	A	U	Z	Y			L		O
7							F						O	N
8			W	H	O	R	E						O	I
9							R						I	D
10	Q		M	A	X	I	S					E	
11	J	A	P	E	D			A	I	T			
12	U	N		T	O	Y	O			W	I	N	
13	K	A	T		E	S	T	R	O	N	E	
14	E	T	A									
15	D		M	A	L	L	E	I					

Joel: 374		David: 315

David's rack: A E G I P S U

Unseen tiles: B D E E E E G I I L N R S T U V ☐

David played PUN (J2, 11), which according to Quackle is the play with the best winning chances—it edges out PUGH (E5, 20). The board had been closed, and without opening it up, David would have had no chance whatsoever to win the game. His play was a *setup*—that is, it created a hook for a tile that he kept in the leave. David's S could have transformed PUN into SPUN for a potentially high-scoring play along the top row. Setups are great if your opponent cannot possibly use them, which wasn't the case in this situation. In fact, I played DEVIOUS (1D) right after David's PUN. Nevertheless, PUN was the right move. We will discuss setups in more detail later. But for now, let's look at one more example of a play that was both a setup and a board opener. This time the opponent could neither use nor block the play.

Mike: 305 | Opponent: 369

Mike's rack: F I N S T U ☐

Unseen tiles: E E I I I M O Q R R T U V V

Mike Wise was the player on the move. His board opening and unblockable setup play was TOW (L2, 6). Two plays later he played FURNISH (1G, 88), which enabled him to come from behind and win the game.

Here is a clever board-opening play found by a Baltimore expert, Richard Silberg. The game is nearing its conclusion, and in order to have any chance of winning, the player who is trailing must play a bingo. The problem is that it is impossible to play a seven-letter bingo on this board, and the playable eight-letter bingos are unlikely: they require that the G, O, U, or the second T of GOUTIEST be played through.

Richard: 283 | Opponent: 348

Richard's rack: A G L O O T T

Silberg's unusual solution was OTTO (7C, 5). The beauty of this move is that it sets up two hook locations: B7 for the L on the rack or the remaining M if it is picked from the bag, and G7 for the last S if it is picked. OTTO also makes it difficult for the opponent to play the Q by blocking the U in GOUTIEST. It makes little difference if you can play the Q if you pick it, because having it on the rack means that you will lose anyway.

In truth OTTO is a desperation move, but that is what is called for here. Quackle's recommended play of GLOAT (D1, 24) puts us 41 points down with eleven tiles in the bag. After opponent's likely 18+ points from 1D to 1H or beyond, or after some other blocking play from 2D to the right or down column F, we would be down around 60 on a desolate board—a sure loss.

Know your opponent

Use knowledge of your opponent's strengths and weaknesses and adapt your playing style to maximize your probability of winning. If your opponent's word knowledge is much greater than yours, try to avoid creating an open board. An open board will contain many high-scoring opportunities, and in such a circumstance a player stronger than you is very likely to outscore you. Try instead to close the board down. This can be accomplished by playing words that don't take hook letters before or after them, by using consonants to close off whole sections of the board to future play, and by making overlapping plays so that the tiles in your play do not extend out into open space.

A closed board makes the two of you more equal. On an open board, it might be possible to create eight-letter bingos through six or seven available letters. No eight-letter bingos might be playable on a tightly closed board. If your opponent knows more of these bingos than you do and/or is better at anagramming long words than you are, you will be more competitive with her if neither of you can put such words on the board. I occasionally lose games to players who are much weaker than I am. This usually occurs over a closed board, and it causes me great frustration.

The stronger player must strive to open the board. He should create openings for hooks (without being too reckless about it), especially if the hook letter changes the existing word into one that the opponent is unlikely to know and a hook tile is retained in the leave. He should play long words, as these can create multiple openings that are difficult to block. He should also try to play to the left and to the upper portions of the board, as these sectors can be more easily blocked off from play by an opponent than can the right and lower portions of the board. By opening them up early, he will make it more difficult for his opponent to strangle play.

It may of course become necessary to reevaluate the adoption of a particular playing style as a game progresses. A player who falls behind early in the game to a stronger player will be insuring defeat by continuing to try to close up the board. Conversely, a player who has achieved a substantial lead over a weaker player should not continue to open the board, but should close it down to protect that lead.

What if your opponent is of approximately the same strength as you? Evenly matched players can have radically different styles. Some, including me, like a wide open, speculative, swashbuckling game. Others consider themselves to be at the mercy of the tile gods in such situations and prefer a tighter board over which they can exercise some semblance of control. If you are versatile enough to feel comfortable on either an open or closed board, you might try steering the game away from the style that your opponent most likes. If you have a strong stylistic preference, however, play in accordance with it. When your opponent's style is similar to your own, do not alter your approach, because you will only irritate both your opponent and yourself. Unless your opponent has a very low tolerance for frustration, you will be no more successful than if you followed your own stylistic inclinations. Your enjoyment of the game will in all likelihood diminish, whatever your opponent's misery threshold happens to be.

Make inferences concerning your opponent's leave

There are two main sources of uncertainty in SCRABBLE. The first is the selection of tiles. The second is the contents of your opponent's rack. Reduce these uncertainties and you will win more games.

The technical term for reducing uncertainty concerning the selection of tiles is cheating. There is no ethical way to control one's tile selection. The technical term for deducing your opponent's rack is prescience (or X-ray vision), which in most of us is oddly lacking. Nevertheless, it is possible to increase one's prescience through a careful examination of a player's preceding move or moves. Consider the following example:

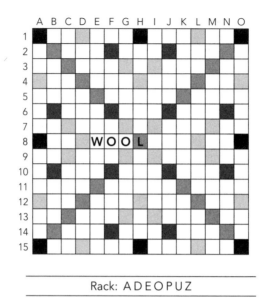

Rack: A D E O P U Z

There are three main alternatives here: OOZED (F8, 35), ZOO (F6, 32), and OUZO (F8, 33). In terms of leave, OUZO is clearly best. Its main drawback is the placement of an O at F11, right next to a double word square. If the opponent has the J, he could easily score 38 points or more on his next turn by making a vertical play from E11. (The 20+ points that would result from playing an H or a W at E11 are not significant enough to deter you from playing OUZO.) The opponent probably does not have the J, however, and this deduction is based on his first play. Had the J been in his opening rack, he would have played JOWL, or something better than JOWL, instead of WOOL. The four replacement tiles after WOOL come from a bag containing eighty-six tiles. As there is only one J in the tile distribution, the probability of his picking the J is less than 5 percent. OUZO is thus a safe bet.

It might be argued that after playing OUZO, the S hook at 12F is dangerous. A play made using it and the double word square at 12D is only likely to score in the high 20s or 30s, however. Furthermore, the probability is that the opponent does not have an S. If he had one in his opening rack, he might have played WOOLS (8D) for the extra 10 points. Given that there are four S's in the tile distribution, he has only about an 18 percent chance of picking at least one of them with his four replacement tiles.

It is at times possible to ascertain whether your opponent is struggling with a bad rack or if she has a great one. If she goes first and exchanges one tile on her opening play, you can be positive that she has bingo-conducive tiles. A low-scoring two-tile opening play is another indication of a good rack. And if she makes an S hook setup play, it is very likely that she has an S.

Here we have the same board position as on page 92, minus the plays of YIN and THUD. It is your opponent's turn, and she plays THUD (7H, 15). From this play you conclude that she has the X but not an A or an O for a big play at 10I. THUD sets up the X for any vowel except an I (AX, EX, OX at 6I; XU at 6J). Better, if she did not have the X, would have been THUD at C5 for an additional 4 points. Knowledge of part of your opponent's rack is often just plain scary rather than useful. Sometimes, however, this information is an important consideration in determining your next play. That is why it is important, crucial even, to do the following as you play:

Keep a record of the tiles that have been played

It is allowable to keep a running written record of the tiles as they have been played during the course of a game. This procedure is called tile tracking. In the late 1970s and early 1980s it was rarely done, but it is now almost universally practiced by tournament players.

The rationale behind tile tracking is not hard to surmise. It enables you to know exactly what tiles your opponent has near the end of the game. In a close game, this information could well be the difference between winning and losing. Tracking can help you earlier in the game as well. If you know, for example, that six of twenty tiles remaining in the bag or on your opponent's rack are I's, you might (correctly) think twice before making a play that expends five of your tiles but not the I on your rack.

Some people object to the whole idea of tile tracking. They feel that players should not have access to a written record of the tiles that have been played. Instead they should develop the ability to track tiles in their heads. Tracking is illegal in most card games, so why should it be allowed in SCRABBLE?

My feeling is that tile tracking enhances play. Moreover, it is unfair to compare the ability to keep a hundred SCRABBLE tiles in your head with the ability to remember only about half as many cards. In a timed game it is virtually impossible for almost any mortal to track tiles accurately without recording them. Tracking improves the quality of play and allows for the calculation of potentially brilliant moves in the endgame that would not otherwise be possible.

Tile tracking has its disadvantages. It takes time away from the consideration of plays, and it may distract one from a careful analysis of the board position. It takes much practice to track an entire game accurately. Common mistakes are forgetting to track one or more plays, recording the same tile twice (most typically by recording the entire word played, not just the letters from the last turn contributing to it), and erroneously recording the letter that a blank represents, rather than recording the blank.

Tiles can be tracked in a number of ways. The player may write down on a blank portion of the score sheet the one hundred tile letters or a symbolic representation of them just after the game has begun. Or a player might use a preprinted list of the tile distribution in order to save the time for recording tiles during the game.

Many players write out letters individually and then cross them off as they are played. Others simply write the letter and the number of tiles of the letter in the distribution after it. When a certain letter is played, the number next to that letter in the player's tracking scheme is crossed off and replaced by the next lower number. The letters need not be listed alphabetically. Some players group their letters according to categories such as vowels, high-point letters, and so forth.

When there are fewer than seven tiles in the bag, it is a good idea to cross off tiles on your rack from your tracking list. You can then write down all the tiles that are still unaccounted for in one place on your score sheet. Shield this portion of the sheet from your opponent, so that your rack cannot be deduced from it. Few of my opponents have ever tried to examine my score sheet. Nevertheless, one might as well be cautious.

One more tip: use your tracking sheet to be aware of the ratio between consonants and vowels that remain unseen to you. This is *very* important, especially in the endgame! Suppose, for example, that there are three tiles in the bag and from your vantage point eight of the ten unseen tiles are vowels. You will want to make a play that conserves your consonants and gets rid of your vowels.

Challenge!

Challenges happen when a player plunks down a word and her opponent doubts its validity. The opponent says "challenge" and the play is then checked to see if it is in the word source. One of the two players then loses a turn.

Losing a turn is a severe penalty. Not only does your opponent get to play twice in a row, he also learns what some or all of your tiles are. Losing a challenge also feels bad. Common sense therefore would seem to dictate that two basic tenets be followed with respect to challenging and bluffing: (1) challenge your opponent's play only when her word is a phony, and (2) never play a phony yourself. These tenets only apply to the idealized case in which both players know the OSPD stone cold, however, and even then strict adherence to them may not always be advisable. For most of us, a good deal more uncertainty is involved. You may not know if the word you are thinking of challenging is allowable, and you may be unsure whether a word you are thinking of playing is allowable and/or whether your opponent will challenge it. I suggest the following:

Bluff only if the payoff from bluffing is considerably greater than the payoff from not bluffing. The loss of a turn is a severe penalty. Don't risk the loss of a turn unless it's well worth it.

On the other hand, challenge a word you are fairly certain is a phony, even if it does not score particularly well. Suppose, for example, that your opponent has played VOD on a double word score for 12 points. You are 98 percent certain that VOD is no good, but you let VOD stay because your opponent scores so little for it. You should definitely challenge in situations like this one. First, 12 points may not seem like much, but it may be the difference between winning and losing. Second, your opponent may be trying to develop her rack. She may have played VOD for the express purpose of getting rid of the V. Maybe she has another V on her rack, or maybe she is building toward a bingo by disposing of her V and keeping bingo-conducive tiles. If the best she can do on this play is 12 points, then the best she is likely to do on her next turn after losing the challenge is about the same. Finally, even if VOD doesn't do anything particularly wonderful for her rack, it should be challenged just to keep your opponent from picking potentially valuable replacement tiles from the bag. And of course it is demoralizing to lose a challenge.

If you are unsure whether a word you are thinking of playing is acceptable, but playing that word is the only way to win, do not hesitate! One of my opponents in a crucial tournament game refrained from playing QUINOL on his next to last play because he wasn't sure if it was good and because it placed the Q in a dangerous position (on A4) with one U still unaccounted for. QUINOL would have been worth 60+ points, and though I had a U, I would not have been able to take advantage of the Q to score well. QUINOL probably would have won the game (and the tournament) for my opponent, and no other play could have done that. Always give yourself a shot at winning. Hmm. Seems like I mentioned this at least once before in this chapter. Consider it a SCRABBLE prime directive.

Definitely challenge a word that you are even the slightest bit unsure of if allowing that word to stand means certain defeat. There are few sadder sights than a losing player who discovers only after the game that her opponent's 120-point play was a phony. The more devastating your opponent's dubious play, the more likely you should be to challenge it.

Consider playing a lucrative phony if you are way behind in the game. Your opponent may not want to risk dissipating a lead by challenging your word incorrectly. He may figure that the only way to lose the game would be to make an incorrect challenge, allowing you a free turn to catch up.

Down 128 points, in the possession of a rack containing BBEISTU and no playable bingos on the board, I took a risk and played TUBBIES for 86 points. I knew that this word was not acceptable, but it gave me a chance to win. I hoped that my opponent would not be absolutely sure of TUBBIES' invalidity. If he were to lose the challenge, I would have the opportunity to make the score really close on my next turn. But by refraining from challenging, he retained a substantial 42-point lead and the move. His chances of winning were still excellent, and given that he did not know if TUBBIES was acceptable, he was correct not to challenge me. As it turned out, I won the game. I almost certainly would have lost it had I not tried this phony.

On the other hand, when losing the challenge is the only way for you to lose the game, refrain from challenging a word unless you are absolutely sure that it is no good. Similarly, if the only way you can lose the game is if your opponent successfully challenges your word, don't play a word you are at all unsure about. Due to the effects of tiredness and tension, it often happens that players self-destruct near the end of a tournament game. Among the most tried and true methods of self-destruction are inappropriate bluffs and challenges. Two games stick in my mind. In one of them, any valid word would have won the game for my opponent. Instead she lost by trying ICER. In another, my expert opponent had a senior moment and played LITA. LATI, TALI, and LITAI are good, but not LITA. Yes, I've done it as well. I once played GLID near the end of a game, which was challenged off. Fortunately, I won that game by 2 points anyway. Don't play phonies at the end of the game!

Phonies are part of the game, and you should play them occasionally to keep your opponents off guard. You don't want to acquire a reputation as a player who never plays phonies, because if you do, no one will ever challenge your acceptable words. So go ahead. Play the occasional phony. Just make your attempt believable. Make it confusable[8] with a real word. It could be a false spelling, an unacceptable "variant," a made-up compound word (e.g., DOGTAG), or an incorrect conjugation, pluralization, or comparative form. Don't try words that appear ridiculous. There are some ridiculous-looking words in the dictionary, but they are so unusual, they are easily remembered by most players. If you play a word like MOXBIB you will lose a turn for sure.

Stephen Fisher, a now retired expert player, was a master of the plausible phony. In one game against me, he got away with SUBANAL. This phony is probably less likely to be challenged by an expert than by a weaker player! The expert may confuse it with SUBALAR, SUBORAL, POSTANAL, and PREANAL, all of which are acceptable. The amateur player may not know these words, and might challenge SUBANAL simply because it looks weird. Plausible phonies may also be "hybrids" of existing words. BILINEAL, for example, sounds correct probably because it is so close to BIENNIAL and BILINEAR. I have played the phony IXTER twice and gotten away with it both times. Reason: it sounds like IXTLE and OXTER, two acceptable words. Phony hybrids are seldom challenged because they are easily confused with acceptable words.

The OSPD provides myriad opportunities for confusion. For example, only one of the following four words is unacceptable. Do you know which it is?

LUGWORM, LUGWORT, LUNGWORM, LUNGWORT

How about the following trio? Which one(s) are phonies?

SALTWORK, SALTWORM, SALTWORT

LUGWORT and SALTWORM are the phonies. The others are all acceptable.

Take the playing strength of your opponent into consideration when deciding whether to challenge or to bluff. It is one thing to challenge an

---

[8] A phony itself, though allowable in World Championship play.

implausible word played by an intermediate player, and another to challenge such a word when played by an expert. Experts like to probe their opponents' vocabularies by playing unusual words early in the game. If they draw unsuccessful challenges, they will continue to play unusual words until their opponents stop challenging. Then they might try a phony or two.

Don't try to bluff an expert unless you enjoy this game as a spectator sport. As obvious as this advice may appear, it is much more common to lose a turn by attempting to play a phony against a stronger player than it is to lose a turn by incorrectly challenging a stronger player. One reason experts are experts is that they know the lexicon.

You are allowed to say "hold" before making your challenge official. Be reflective; take advantage of holding. Take your time, then decide whether to challenge. Also, don't challenge a word without examining how placement of the word on the board might affect the game. Sometimes it is to your advantage to leave your opponent's phony on the board. The word may provide an opening for your bingo where previously there had been none. It may, on the other hand, close down the board. If you have a substantial lead, your opponent's unchallenged phony may guarantee your victory!

You also may want to set a trap for the opponent. If the phony word looks like a noun, for example, and you have reason to suspect that your opponent has retained an S or a blank on his rack, you may wish to refrain from challenging until and if your opponent pluralizes his phony. Or you may wish to pluralize his phony yourself—but do this only if you have a strong sense that your opponent is convinced that his play is good. It's risky to do this, especially as SCRABBLE players are good actors. I once played HENBITE in a club game. My opponent did not challenge this ridiculous nonword, perhaps because he confused it with HENBIT (which is in the OSPD) or perhaps because of my reputation for playing obscure but acceptable words. He tried a bingo on his next turn, in the process of which he hooked an -S onto HENBITE. He was not amused when I challenged HENBITES and his bingo off the board.

If an expert plays an obviously phony word, there is a chance that she may actually want you to challenge her. This ploy usually occurs at the beginning of the game. Let's say, for example, that your opponent goes first and has AEIORST on her rack. She will probably exchange the O, retaining the famous SATIRE leave discussed in the previous chapter. This is the best she can do by far, even though it scores no points, cedes the double word score to you, and puts you on notice that your opponent is bingo hunting. Alternatively, your opponent might try a creative phony such as AORTI or RATOI. Don't be fooled into thinking that she has accidentally used an incorrect plural form of AORTA or has misspelled RATIO. She probably wants you to challenge this play. From her point of view, if you don't challenge, she gets 12 points and a nice ES leave. If you do challenge, she may be able to play an eight-letter bingo through one of the tiles in your first play. You most definitely should challenge her play, but afterward you should seriously consider exchanging tiles or playing defensively on your opening move. I was a victim of this ploy a couple of years ago. Joel Sherman played HURD on his first move. I challenged it off, which is what Joel wanted me to do. I then made a play using an E, and Joel's next play was DRUTHERS. I felt like an idiot all game.

A rarely used but potentially helpful resource is the "fake challenge." This refers to the purposeful challenge of a word that the challenger knows is acceptable. If you hold bingo-conducive tiles and your opponent plays an unusual word but one that you know is allowable, you might consider challenging in the hope that your opponent's next play will open the board for your bingo. The challenge disguises your intentions. If you instead simply pass, your opponent will realize that you have good tiles. He could then either play defensively, exchange tiles to improve his rack, or pass if he was leading in the game. If he was behind, you could pass again after his pass, forcing him to play in order to avoid losing by the consecutive pass rule (six non-scoring plays in a row and either player can demand that the game end).

The purposeful phony and the fake challenge can both be used to advantage in the endgame as well. Imagine, for example, that there are few tiles left in the bag, the Q has not been played, and the board position and remaining unseen tiles are such that whoever draws the Q will be unable to play it away.

You are losing by 10 or so points. You would like to pass to avoid picking the Q, but if you do so your opponent is likely to follow suit. Your opponent plays an obscure word that you know is acceptable, and you challenge him in the hope that he will make another play afterward rather than pass. As a consequence of his second play, he will draw at least one more tile than he would have, had you not challenged him. You have thus increased his chances of picking the Q by making an "incorrect" challenge. If the same conditions exist but it is your turn to play, you might play a purposefully phony word in the hope that your opponent will challenge you, make a play, and draw the Q as his reward.

Don't bluff a phony bingo with seven or fewer tiles in the bag, unless your play is absolutely essential for you to have any chance of winning the game. An unsuccessful bingo bluff near the end of the game can be very damaging. In addition to losing your turn, your opponent will be able to deduce the tiles in the bag. She can then determine whether she should play away many or few tiles, more vowels than consonants or the reverse, and what specific tiles should be played away in order to avoid tile duplication.

Setups

A setup is a play that changes the board position so that the player making the setup will be able to use the tiles in his leave to great advantage. In order for a setup to be effective, the probability that the opponent will be able to use or block the opening created by it must be small. Also, the player must not sacrifice too much in order to make the setup. The total number of points scored for the setup and its culmination must be greater than what the player would be likely to garner over the same two turns had a setup not been prepared.

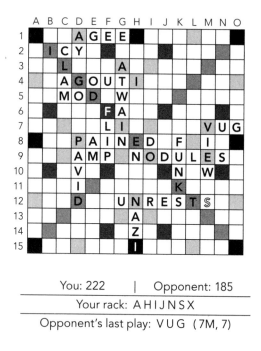

	A	B	C	D	E	F	G	H	I	J	K	L	M	N	O
1				A	G	E	E								
2		I	C	Y											
3			L				A								
4			A	G	O	U	T	I							
5			M	O	D		W								
6					F	A									
7					L	I						V	U	G	
8			P	A	I	N	E	D		F		I			
9			A	M	P		N	O	D	U	L	E	S		
10			V					N		W					
11			I					K							
12			D		U	N	R	E	S	T	S				
13							A								
14							Z								
15							I								

You: 222 | Opponent: 185

Your rack: A H I J N S X

Opponent's last play: V U G (7M, 7)

The opponent's last play indicates that he is fishing for a bingo to get back in the game: he creates a new opening, making it impossible for you to block both it and the openings along rows 14 and 15. In addition, he is probably dispensing with his two least bingo-conducive tiles. Why else would he make a play producing such an opening that scores only 7 points?

As you cannot block both of his openings, you go about the business of scoring lots of points while taking the more dangerous opening at O8. HANGS (O4, 39) is the highest scoring play you can find, but much finer is JIGS (O5, 36). It sacrifices 3 points and uses one tile less than HANGS, but prepares a 50-point X play at N6 (XI/XU) next turn. This setup can be blocked, but not very easily. Also, it doesn't look like a setup. Your opponent may think that you are simply making the best play you can find, perhaps the only one available to you that uses the J and the triple word square. As a result, he might not feel the necessity to block the opening, even if he could.

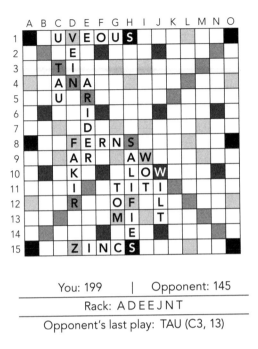

	A	B	C	D	E	F	G	H	I	J	K	L	M	N	O
1		U	V	E	O	U	S								
2			E												
3		T	I												
4		A	N	A											
5		U	R												
6			I												
7			D												
8		F	E	R	N	S									
9		A	R			A	W								
10		K			L	O	W								
11		I		T	I	T	I								
12		R		O	F		L								
13		M	I		T										
14				E											
15		Z	I	N	C	S									

You: 199 | Opponent: 145

Rack: A D E E J N T

Opponent's last play: TAU (C3, 13)

Stephen Fisher played this beauty against me many years ago: NANA (4B, 4). NANA set up the J at 4A, as JNANA is an OSPD-acceptable word. A J play using one of the triple word scores at A1 or A8 would be worth a barrelful of points.

Stephen's setup theoretically could have been blocked by LATI, SATI, YETI, SITI, or TITI (all at 3A). It might have been partially blocked by a word using the -S or -T hook at C6. I did not have these resources, and on his second play following NANA, Stephen played EJECTA (A3, 89). A Quackle simulation found NANA to be more than 11 points better than the next best play, JAR (9C, 18), and it was 12 points better than TAJ (C11, 24).

	A	B	C	D	E	F	G	H	I	J	K	L	M	N	O
1		L													
2		I	F												
3		B	E	N				C	A	M	E	O	E	D
4			N	A								T			
5				R							P	A			
6				R							E				
7				O	F		J	A	K	E	S				
8				W	A	V	E	R			T	A	C	E	T
9					I		T				L		E		
10	W	O	R	R	I	E	D				E		N		
11				Y							S		T		
12													R		
13													A		
14			D	E	M	I	R	E	P				L		
15	V	I	O	L				H	A	U	G	H	S		

Stephen: 269 | Dee: 360

Rack: B O Q S T U Z

Opponent's last play: VIOL (15A, 30)

The brilliant desperation setup play of TOD (O1, 12) was also made by Stephen Fisher. Down by 91 to Dee Segrest, he needed a big score to get back in the game, and this play gave him that possibility.

Dee played YONI (J10) on her next turn. That was fine with Stephen, because the play he was hoping to set up with TOD was not blocked: BEZIQUE (N2, 102)! All he needed to play it was to pick one of the four remaining I's among the nineteen unseen tiles. His chance of drawing at least one I in his two replacement tiles was 39 percent. As it turned out, he drew an I, played BEZIQUE, but lost the game by 4 points.

A Quackle simulation of the position has TOD at least 7 points in front of all plays scoring 30 or more points. Only BO (J10, 22) was close at 4 points back, probably because it keeps both the Q and the Z for separate big plays.

Setups aren't made solely for the purpose of scoring as many points as possible. They can be used to help you get rid of undesirable tiles or to play out before the opponent does. We will examine how setups can become very important in the endgame a little later.

Q Strategy

Before 1991, the Q was the queen of spades of SCRABBLE. Picking it out of the bag without one of the four U's in a SCRABBLE set was like being stuck with the licorice Chuckles, only worse. But in 1991, QAT was added to the OSPD, and fifteen years later QI was admitted to the lexicon. The addition of this one word has gone a long way toward defanging the Q.

It remains the case that the Q is a pathetic tile if not accompanied by a U. There are only fifteen words, not counting standard plurals, that contain a Q but no U: FAQIR, QABALA, QABALAH, QADI, QAID, QANAT, QAT, QI, QINDAR, QINTAR, QOPH, QWERTY, SHEQALIM, SHEQEL, and TRANQ. This makes the Q so unwieldy that a common problem for the player with the U-less Q is whether to exchange it or not.

The greater the number of U's already played, the more readily you should consider exchanging the Q. This assumes that the U's played are inaccessible for your Q. The rationale for this guideline is obvious: the fewer U's in the bag, the lower the probability that you will pick one. Consider the situation critical if three U's are showing on the board.

The greater the number of points by which you are losing, the more ready you should be to exchange the Q. The U-less Q does more than prevent you from playing bingos. It lessens the probability of making high-scoring non-bingo plays, as you have only six tiles to work with rather than the full seven. If you have a lead or if the game is close, holding on to the Q may not be so critical. If you are falling behind, however, you cannot afford the Q. You must exchange it in order to have a realistic hope of catching up.

The tighter the board is, the more readily should you exchange the Q. If the board is completely closed down, it might be wise to exchange the Q even if you have a U accompanying it. It makes no sense to keep the Q if there is no place to play it.

The fewer tiles from your rack that a play you are considering making dispenses with, the greater should be your readiness to exchange the Q rather than make that play. If you only get to pick a few replacement tiles, you will not have much chance of pulling a U. Try to play away at least four tiles in lieu of exchanging the Q.

It makes little sense to retain an unplayable Q on your rack if your other tiles cannot be combined to form a high-scoring play. I almost always exchange in such situations if I am unable to find a play worth at least 20 points, and I know of other experts whose tipping point is much higher— closer to 30 points.

If the game is nearing its end, the U's are gone, and there is no open I for QI, exchanging the Q should be a top priority. Don't risk the chance that your opponent will play away enough tiles so that fewer than seven will remain in the bag, for then you will no longer have the option of exchanging the Q.

These guidelines are meant to be broken occasionally. In fact it is rare that at least one of them is not violated by either the best available play or by exchanging. If you are able to score a great number of points without using the Q, for example, you would probably be wise to ignore any of the first four guidelines. If such a play violates all of these guidelines, however, it had better be a blockbuster.

On the other hand, don't develop too strong a hatred for the Q. It is neither correct to rid yourself of the Q at all costs, nor to play for as many points as possible without regard to how the Q may cripple your future point production. Each situation must be evaluated individually.

If you have the QU combination on your rack and you are bent on getting rid of the Q as quickly as possible, you may overlook plays that separate your U from your Q. Sometimes, however, your best play requires you to do this. Consider the opening rack of BCENQUZ. No QU plays are available, and the Z cannot be played without also playing the U. This means that you must resign yourself to a maximum of 10 points (BEN, NEB) in order to retain the QU combination. If you play ZEBU, however, you score 30 points. There is considerable risk that your opponent may make a play that prevents you from placing the Q above the U on your next play. Nevertheless, ZEBU (8F, 8G, or 8H) simulates 8 to 10 points higher than BEN or NEB. Don't reject a play like it simply because you wouldn't dream of parting with the QU combination.

One more comment concerning the U-less Q: keep in mind that the U-less Q words use a lot of the same letters, in particular the A, D, I, N, and T. For example, if you have the Q and a T on your rack, consider making plays that keep the T, if they don't entail too much of a sacrifice compared with other plays that spend it. Because A's are so plentiful, you stand a good chance of picking at least one of them, or one may be open for you on the board.

Rack: D N O O Q R V

Your highest-scoring play is DOR (11C, 32). However, your second-highest-scoring play NOR (11C, 29) is better. It conserves the D, for a sacrifice of only 3 points. With none of the nine I's yet showing on the board, you stand a decent chance of drawing one even though you will be picking only three tiles. NOR thus allows you the distinct possibility of playing QAID or QADI at F7 on your next play. Furthermore, your opponent is highly unlikely to block this spot, given the other more interesting openings on the board.

Finally, you should keep the U-less Q words in mind *even when* you have the QU combination on your rack. Understandably enough, many players overlook this possibility.

Exchanging tiles

The exchange is a useful option for simultaneously dispensing with undesirable tiles and for increasing the probability of picking desirable tiles.

The forfeiture of a scoring opportunity is a severe penalty, so you should not exchange unless it is absolutely necessary. An exchange is justified only when the points that could have been taken instead of exchanging are more than made up for on subsequent turns. This occurs less often than one might think.

On average, I exchange tiles about once every thirty plays. I almost always exchange five or more tiles, though sometimes only one or two. An exchange of four tiles or fewer usually indicates a fishing play, whereas an exchange of five or more tiles indicates a horrid rack that must be returned to the bag. I exchange when my tiles are really poor (e.g., AAIOUUV, BCFNPPW, etc.), or when I feel that I have an excellent chance to convert a one- or two-tile fishing play into a bingo.

Don't shrink from exchanging when it is really necessary to do so. I occasionally watch novice and intermediate players compete, and it seems to me that some of them must consider exchanging tiles to be an almost shameful act. I have seen such players make 6-point plays that leave five vowels on the rack! Alfred Butts once said that in all his years of playing SCRABBLE he never once exchanged tiles. Then again, he never played in tournaments.

The endgame

The endgame in SCRABBLE is the most complicated, difficult, and treacherous stage of the game. It is at this point that one's efforts for the better part of an hour can be kissed good-bye with one wrong play. It is virtually impossible for anyone to play perfect endgames, and in fact making up rules for how endgames should be played invites counterexamples. Nevertheless, I'll go out on the limb. Here are some guidelines that may help:

Strive to play out first

In a close game, the player who plays out usually wins. Twice the total value of the opponent's remaining tiles is added to the score, and this bonus often provides the margin of victory. In such situations, it is therefore more important to make a play that enables you to go out on your next turn than it is to make a higher-scoring play that doesn't allow you to do this.

	A	B	C	D	E	F	G	H	I	J	K	L	M	N	O
1								W							D
2								A							I
3	V	I	E					L							N
4		F	L	Y				E							G
5			E	P	E	I	R	I	C				O	E
6		Y	O	W					H				S	H	
7									I				T		
8				J	A	R	G	O	N	S		B	A	N	I
9			C	O	X		R						T		
10		Z		L		B	E						U		
11		O		T		O	E						R		
12		N		E			N				M	E			
13	Q	A	I	D			L			V	I	S	A		
14	U	T			E	K	E					G			
15	A	E		P	L	A	T	F	O	R	M	S			

You: 415 | Opponent: 420

Your rack: A A D D O T U

Opponent's rack: E I N R U

Here it is possible to score 23 points with ANTED (12A), 18 points with DADA (L3) or TAV (A1), and 17 points with DAD (7A). All of these moves lose, because they don't address the opponent's threats to play out: INURED or RUINED (1J) and LUNIER (3H).

The correct play is AOUDAD (2H). Though AOUDAD scores only 10 points, it both prevents your opponent from playing out and guarantees that you can play out and win the game on your next turn with ANTE (12A, 21), after your opponent's best play of REIN (2B, 23).

Players often start off their endgames by going for the highest-scoring play. Sometimes, however, it is better to do the opposite. It all depends on which play ends the game sooner.

Your rack: E G L N O O T
Opponent's rack: A D E I T

The best play is GENET (L1, 8). Why? Because it retains the letters needed to play LOO (14A, 23), which ends the game and cannot be blocked. Opponent's best play is then LATED (L9, 16), and we follow with LOO for a net score of +17. If we had started with LOO or GOO, we would not have done so well. We cannot play out if opponent blocks GENET, say with DIET (3L, 13). After opponent's GAM (E3, 12) on his next turn, we always net less than the 17 points we would have netted by playing GENET first.

Your rack: A D D E N S T

Opponent's rack: B E I O R

The "obvious" high-scoring play of WEANS (H11, 32) is an error because it doesn't guarantee the out-in-two. Opponent can play out with REBOIL (C10, 16), and after collecting another twelve from our rack, our net is only +4. Or if opponent is razor sharp, he can play ORIBI (8A, 30) followed by REFORMATES (I5, 15), making WEANS look even worse. Best is TEDDED (9A, 11), followed by ANES (K9, 18). If opponent makes his best play in between, OBE (14A, 24), our net is +9.

Don't empty the bag

This advice is golden. With just a few tiles in the bag, it is amazing how frequently the best play is the one that leaves a tile or two in the bag rather than the one that empties it.

Emptying the bag gives a player perfect knowledge of his opponent's rack. This is a significant advantage, as the player might be able to use such knowledge to guarantee an out-in-two for himself, or to block his opponent's best continuations.

If you have a substantial lead, the tiles unseen are bingo-conducive, and you cannot close all the bingo alleys, leaving at least one tile in the bag becomes doubly imperative. Doing so will enable you to make at least one more play, should your opponent actually play the bingo. The points you garner from that additional play are in effect worth double: they add to your score, and the value of the tiles used in making the play will not contribute to your opponent's score. It is sometimes worth it to pass your turn just to be certain that you will have a play, should your opponent play a bingo.

Here is an example in which I did not follow my own advice:

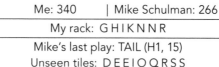

Me: 340 | Mike Schulman: 266

My rack: G H I K N N R

Mike's last play: TAIL (H1, 15)
Unseen tiles: D E E I O Q R S S

How to Play SCRABBLE Like a Champion

I learned a painful lesson from this game. With two tiles in the bag, I played away three with HUNK (D2, 22). I picked the Q and D from the bag, and Mike played SOIREES (N5, 73), ending the game. After the dust cleared, I had an 11-point loss.

Before playing HUNK, I had a 74-point lead and could not lose unless Mike played a bingo. Moreover, the Q could not be one of the letters in the bingo, because with the open U available at D3, no combination of the other letters formed a playable bingo with the Q. I should not have emptied the bag. Instead, I should have reasoned out this situation as follows:

1. I will lose if I make a play that empties the bag, sticking myself with the Q, and if Mike plays a bingo. I might even lose if I make a one-tile play that does not empty the bag, such as HEH (M13, 28), as I might pick the Q and be unable to play it away on my next turn.

2. If Mike has the Q on his rack and needs to play it before bingoing, he must play at least two other tiles away with it, except for SUQ (D2, 24), which would result in his last rack consisting of DEEIORS. Although these letters combine to form both OREIDES and OSIERED, Mike would not have a bingo playable on this board with them.

Conclusion: Passing my turn guarantees the win.

I also would have won with KNOWING (D8, 40) or HOWKING (D9, 40), which would have put me too far ahead for Mike to catch up. Nevertheless, passing would probably have resulted in a substantially larger cushion than these moves.

Here is another example where passing one's turn appears to be called for. It is from a tournament game I played early in 2010 against Will Anderson. It is Will's turn, and he can play OILSEED in two spots (15H, 81, and O9, 75). He will lose only if the Z is in the bag, because in that case I will follow OILSEED with RETAINED (1H, 80). If Will instead passes first and I then play RETAINED, he will win by playing out with OILSEED.

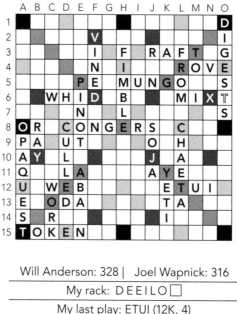

Will Anderson: 328 | Joel Wapnick: 316

My rack: D E E I L O ☐

My last play: ETUI (12K, 4)
Unseen tiles: A E E I N R T Z

The situation is more intriguing than it appears on the surface, however, because given the unseen tile pool, I am threatening ZAIRE (N10, 68) in addition to the bingo! ZAIRE scores more than enough to win and it eliminates both locations for OILSEED. ZAIRE in fact would leave Will without a playable bingo, and he would lose for sure. It is even possible that if I didn't have the tiles to play ZAIRE, I might win anyway, with a lower-scoring Z play down row N.

Note that Will must choose between passing and playing OILSEED. He cannot try a play such as ER (J2, 4), which empties the bag but blocks

RETAINED and gives himself another shot at OILSEED (at 1G), should he draw an E after I play ZAIRE. This ploy doesn't work because if I had the tiles to play RETAINED, I would follow Will's ER with GRATINEE (G8) instead of ZAIRE.

My previous play of ETUI unfortunately gave Will no idea whether I had the Z or not, as it might have been seen by him as a setup for ZAIRE or as a simple rack balancing play. Nevertheless, I picked two out of three tiles remaining in the bag. He thus should have concluded that it was more likely than not that I had the Z on my rack and that playing OILSEED immediately was called for. He made the right play by playing OILSEED, but fortunately for me the Z was in the bag. The moral of the story, other than that it is sometimes better to be lucky than good, is that before deciding to pass one's turn, look around to be sure that your opponent can't beat you in some surprising way after the pass.

If you think that your opponent is about to play a bingo, leave one tile in the bag rather than leaving more than one tile

I wish someone had reminded me of this before the fourth game of my World Championship finals match in 1993. It is *much* better for you if your opponent draws a single tile from the bag after playing a bingo, rather than if he draws two or three tiles. It is likely that he will score more points with those tiles on his next (and likely last) play than if he were to take only a solitary tile from the bag. It is hard to score many points with one tile.

Think setups

Be alert to endgame setup plays. Try to retain tiles that prevent your opponent from preparing setups, and try to prepare setups for yourself. The endgame is particularly prone to these kinds of plays. With many tiles already on the board, positions often crystallize in such a way that there are what can best be described as nooks and crannies all over the place. These are small closed-off areas within which clever little setup plays can be devised and then executed. Setups are especially effective when the opposing player has fewer than seven tiles on the rack but cannot play out on his next turn. Your opponent's lack of tiles may make it impossible for him to block your setup.

Jim: 349 | Robin: 389

Jim rack: E O T

Robin's rack: Z

In this game between Robin Pollock-Daniel and Jim Kramer, Robin is stuck with the Z. That will be worth 20 points when Jim finally ends the game by playing out, and as Jim is losing by 40, he needs to garner 21 points from his three tiles to win. He played his three tiles separately to earn the tie: WET (G11, 7), HE (2N, 7), and FOE (G3, 6). However, he could have won by 2 points had he seen the setup play of FEE (G3, 6). FEE creates ROT (6E, 16) for his next turn.

	A	B	C	D	E	F	G	H	I	J	K	L	M	N	O
1	J	A	G					D	E	C	E	A	S	E	D
2		N						U			H	E	I	R	
3		A	Z	O				I							
4		N		P	L	O	T	T	E	R					
5		A							O						
6					V	E	I	L	S						
7									A						
8			F	U	R	R	I	E	R						
9				L					I						
10			T	A	B				E				G		
11		C	O	X	A		S	E	N	S	O	R	I	A	
12	A	H	O	Y				M		W	O		M		
13	D	I	T					E		N	U		E	F	
14	I	N					E	L	K		E		D	O	
15	T							R			N			B	

You: 390 | Opponent: 408

Your rack: I P Q U W Y

Opponent's rack: G T V

Opponent's last play: ELK (14H, 17)

Here is an example of how a resourceful player can create a setup to play out. The situation seems hopeless. Not only are you 18 points down, but your opponent seemingly has prevented you from unloading the Q with her last play (you could have played PIQUE, 14D, or QUEY, 14F, had she not played ELK). Then you study the board very carefully and find the winning play: YAW (7I, 23)! The beauty of this play is that it sets up a -P hook at L7 for QUIP (L4, 42) next turn.

Our final example comes from a tournament game between Joel Sherman and me:

	Joel S: 362		Joel W: 382

Joel S's rack: A A D E J L P
Joel W's rack: C I M N O

Joel W's last play: TEXT (13G, 41)

Joel S found the beautiful setup LAND (15B, 5) after the game was over. ELAND is in the OSPD, so LAND would have guaranteed a win by threatening to go out either with JAPE (A12, 81) or JAPER (N6, 30).

CHAPTER 6

Tournament Preparation

Perhaps you are not interested in playing in tournaments. You may dislike the pressure of competition or you may think that you are not good enough to compete. Relax. No matter how badly you play (or think you play), you will begin to notice strength and skill you may not have recognized in yourself before—especially when you find yourself winning against other competitors.

Tournaments can be fun, if you go in with the right attitude. The first thing to realize is that no matter how good you are, you will not win all the time. There is too much luck in SCRABBLE for that. The game's leading money winner, Brian Cappelletto, finished worse than first in 75 of his last 100 tournaments. If you are rated somewhere in the middle of your division and there are twenty players in it, it doesn't take a math genius to understand that the likelihood is great that you will not win. Don't expect to. Instead, come in with the attitude that your entry fee covers a day or more of intense intellectual stimulation.

Second, don't confuse your SCRABBLE rating with your personal worth. Not only is a rating just a number, it is a very unstable number. Ratings bounce around a lot. If you are new to tournament SCRABBLE, your rating likely will go up for a while. Then it will stabilize. For most people, what follows is random noise. SCRABBLE ratings go up and they come back down. If you want to feel good when yours goes up and bad when it goes down, be my guest. Just remember that your rating no longer will be moving in one direction.

You meet interesting people at SCRABBLE tournaments. There is a lot of diversity in our microcosm. Players come in all sizes, races, ages, sexual orientations, political stripes, ethnic groups, and personalities. But because of the nature of SCRABBLE, players are generally more educated and intelligent than most people. In addition, most of us try to make newcomers feel welcome. We understand that it is in our interest to be supportive of beginners, as the vitality of tournament life can be maintained only by a constant infusion of new blood.

Tournaments last from one to five days, with most of them taking up both a Saturday and a Sunday. A typical tournament day consists of six to eight games, broken up by lunch. Often tournaments are held in nice places or at resort hotels, which makes them a unique combination of vacation and intense mental activity. One of the nicest aspects of tournaments is getting together with friends in the evening for a good dinner and conversation. Some players prefer to play some casual SCRABBLE. Others might go out on the town (if there is one), study words, read a book, relax, or do whatever else appeals to them. A tournament adds the perfect amount of structure to a mini-vacation. And of course it's also an escape: no laundry to do, no kids to care for, no meals to prepare, no supermarket shopping, and no business to attend to. Sounds nice, doesn't it?

Most tournaments these days run multiple divisions. The separation of players by ability pretty much ensures that you will neither be overwhelmed nor unchallenged by your opposition. Pairing systems additionally maximize the likelihood that you will compete against players whose abilities are roughly equal to yours, as you likely will be playing people who have won-lost records similar to yours.

The remainder of this chapter presents methods for effectively improving your game through anagram practice, dictionary study, memorization, and game playing. The following chapter deals with playing behavior: what proper etiquette entails, what you can do when you are not playing SCRABBLE in order to stay in top playing shape, and behaviors to avoid if you wish to play your best.

Preparation

How well one does in a tournament is not solely dependent on raw talent. Natural ability helps, of course, but study and training are very important. David Prinz won $1,500 for placing first in the 1978 SCRABBLE North American Championship.[9] To give you an idea of how important study was to his victory, he estimated that his prize money averaged out to about 15 cents per hour of total training time. Joe Edley won the second Nationals by studying the OSPD three hours a day, seven days a week, for two years. I did not put in quite as much effort to win the 1983 Nationals, though I did work consistently and diligently for well over a year.

Although a high degree of dedication, time, and effort is necessary to be competitive with the best players in the game, you can become quite a decent player with much less effort. If you attend club sessions on a regular basis for about half a year, you will learn a tremendous amount. You will know all of the two-letter words, many of the threes and fours, some of the fives, and a sprinkling of unusual seven- and eight-letter bingos. In addition, your general playing ability will improve markedly.

If you wish to be an expert, it is necessary to spend time studying and training. I differentiate between these terms. *Study* refers to efforts intended to increase your playing vocabulary, whereas *training* deals with the development of playing skills such as anagramming, board resourcefulness, and strategic prowess.

General preparation

It is well known that many chess grandmasters keep themselves physically fit so that they can think clearly for long periods of time. The same applies to tournament play in SCRABBLE. Chess masters often must concentrate for as long as five hours at a stretch. SCRABBLE players are not required to do this, but in a tournament such as the Nationals they have to play seven games over a ten-hour period, for four days in a row. Despite breaks for meals and short periods between games, such a schedule is grueling. The level of play declines

---

[9] In different years this tournament has been called the North American Championship and the U.S. SCRABBLE Open, but today is referred to as the Nationals or as the National SCRABBLE Championship.

as the day progresses, and the number of blunders and oversights increases. The rate of decline in the level of play is slower, however, for the player who is physically fit than it is for the player who is out of shape.

It isn't necessary to run ten miles a day, play one-on-one full-court basketball for an hour, and then top that off with an arduous weight-training program in order to play an excellent game of SCRABBLE. What is helpful is a program of moderate and regular exercise. For me, this consists of about 45 minutes of jogging four to five times a week, during which time I rehearse a 16,000-word list of bingos. There are other more enjoyable forms of exercise that you might choose instead.

Exercise is, of course, only a part of physical fitness. The other components include good nutrition, sufficient sleep, low intake of alcohol, and avoidance of smoking. Smoking is not permitted at SCRABBLE tournaments, and many habitual smokers have a difficult time over the board without their cigarettes.

Like many players, I have a lot of difficulty sleeping on tournament nights. It is too easy to ruminate on a game that got away or to think about how crucially important it is to get to sleep *right now* in order to play well tomorrow. A strategy that works moderately well for me is to stay in bed and think something like: *Oh, well. Rest is good too. I'll just lie here with my eyes closed and get as much rest as I can.* There are of course various pharmaceutical remedies for SCRABBLE-induced insomnia, but they may make you drowsy the following morning.

It is good to feel unharried during the period leading up to an important tournament. I try to arrange my life so that I don't have to fight for study and training time. If that is impossible, I try to budget a smaller amount of daily time for preparation over a longer pre-tournament period. It is good to avoid cramming. The pressure to absorb a lot of material over a short period of time can be counterproductive. It can cause confusion and insecurity.

A few of the top players, myself included, practice meditation regularly. Meditation with deep, controlled, slow breathing has two major beneficial effects. First, it provides the mental discipline to ignore stimulation extraneous to the task at hand. When players panic, they ruminate about losing, bad luck, "if only" situations, and so forth. Meditation is an effective way to lower the frequency of such thoughts. It enables one to focus exclusively on one thing only: the game situation. Second, meditation keeps you mentally sharp, as the deep breathing associated with it facilitates the flow of oxygen to the brain.

You don't have to go to school in order to meditate. First, make yourself comfortable in a pleasant, quiet environment. Breathe in deeply and slowly through your nose, and then exhale slowly through your mouth. Try to think of nothing but the pace of your breathing. Meditate for a couple of minutes the first few days, and then gradually increase the time until you are meditating for about half an hour a day (one thirty-minute session or two fifteen-minute sessions). Consider yourself accomplished if you are able to focus exclusively on your breathing and if you feel free and relaxed during the process. When you have reached this point, try meditating in a variety of places and at a variety of times during the day.

Word study

All words are not equally useful. Some can be played to advantage only very rarely, perhaps in less than one game out of a thousand. Others pop up all the time. Even if your ultimate goal is to master the entire dictionary, you might as well start with the words that you are most likely to play rather than ones you will rarely see on the board. The most useful words include:

WORDS OF FIVE LETTERS OR LESS. The vast majority of plays made over the SCRABBLE board are of words that are five letters or less. Knowledge of these words is vital for doing well in tournament play. Fortunately, there are not that many of them. The total number of allowable two- to five-letter words in the OSPD is around 10,000. Many of these are familiar words, and many others are -S plurals that need not be studied separately from their singular forms. If you are a beginning player, there are probably only about 5,000 two- to five-letter words that you need to work on.

BINGOS CONTAINING FEWER THAN TWO HIGH-POINT TILES. About two-fifths of the seven- and eight-letter words listed in the OSPD include at most one tile worth 3 or more points. Because of the tile distribution in SCRABBLE, however, these words account for about four times as many played bingos as do all of the other seven- and eight-letter words. It is conceivable that a word like IDEATION might be played twice in the same session. In fact, it was once played against me twice in the same game. On the other hand, it is unlikely that anyone anywhere will ever play COBWEBBY.

WORDS OF FIVE OR MORE LETTERS CONTAINING FOUR OR MORE VOWELS. Words with many vowels in them are often difficult to find over the board. They are unlikely to have regular prefixes and suffixes, and they often do not sound like they are spelled. They are very common in SCRABBLE play, however, and this is due to the two factors mentioned earlier: the large number of vowels in the tile pool, and the relative ease with which consonants can be played away. Here are all of the five-letter words with four vowels: AALII, ADIEU, AECIA, AERIE, AIOLI, AQUAE, AREAE, AUDIO, AURAE, AUREI, COOEE, EERIE, LOOIE, LOUIE, MIAOU, OIDIA, OORIE, OURIE, QUEUE, URAEI, and ZOEAE. And here are all the seven-letter bingos with five vowels: ABOULIA, ACEQUIA, AECIDIA, AENEOUS, AEOLIAN, AEONIAN, AEROBIA, ALIENEE, AMOEBAE, ANAEMIA, AQUARIA, AQUEOUS, AREOLAE, AUREATE, AUREOLA, AUREOLE, AURORAE, COUTEAU, EPINAOI, EUCAINE, EUGENIA, EULOGIA, EUPNOEA, EVACUEE, EXUVIAE, IPOMOEA, MIAOUED, NOUVEAU, OOGONIA, OUABAIN, OUGUIYA, ROULEAU, SEQUOIA, TAENIAE, URAEMIA, and ZOOECIA.

HOOK WORDS. As demonstrated in Chapter 4, words that can be changed into other words by hooking a letter before or after them are especially useful to know. If your opponent plays PLINK, knowing UPLINK may be helpful. If she plays ONIUM, it might be nice for you to know about IONIUM or GONIUM.

WORDS THAT CANNOT BE PLURALIZED WITH AN S. There are quite a few words in the OSPD that cannot be pluralized but which convey an aura of S-plural plausibility. No one of course would tack an S onto RICH or ACHY. On the other hand, there are hundreds of words like ORAD, TOOM, COUDE, and WAUGH. It is essential to know that these words do not have allowable S pluralizations, both to set traps for the opponent and to avoid playing phonies that risk being challenged off the board.

LISTS. Now that you know which words to study, you are probably wondering where to find them. Many experts spend endless hours constructing word lists. My own lists total 425 typed pages, but that is nothing compared to John O'Laughlin. All of his lists combined total up to more pages than a dozen historical novels.

List-making no longer needs to be tedious. There are now numerous sources that provide lists and books of lists. There are also locations on the Internet from which you can generate your own lists, and there is study software such as Michael Thelen's Zyzzyva that will generate custom lists for you.

How to study

After you have chosen the words that you would like to master, you must apply some sort of systematic method for learning them. Three important approaches for accomplishing this are word recognition, memorization, and anagramming.

WORD RECOGNITION. Unfamiliar words require repeated presentations to be fully absorbed. When I was preparing for the 1983 Nationals, part of my study consisted of spending about an hour a day reading lists of all bingos that I chose not to memorize. I read only a small portion of these lists each day, but after three months I had covered all of them seven or eight times over. I knew the many thousands of words on the lists solidly, and this knowledge was the difference between defeat and victory in at least three of my tournament games.

You can learn words through recognition by simply reading the OSPD over and over again. On your first time through, use a highlighting pen to underline the words you don't know. Your study time will be spent more efficiently on subsequent passes through the dictionary, as you will not be attending to words that you already know.

Another valuable method for increasing word recognition is to prepare cassette tapes, CDs, or iPod files so that you can study at home, on the way to work, in your car, or anywhere else. Make sure that you pronounce each word clearly, and that you spell it out. You may also wish to include the word's definition, what part of speech it is, and if its forms are irregular.

MEMORIZATION. Memorization differs from recognition in that it requires a series of words from a list to be recalled in sequence. Its advantage over recognition is that memorized words are learned with much greater security.

They are rarely forgotten. Another plus is that memorized words can be recalled without having to rely upon anagrammatic skill. This is important, as few players have perfect anagrammatic ability, especially with the eight-letter words. Third, memorization helps you recognize phonies readily. If your opponent plays a word that should be at a certain place in your list but is not there, you can challenge the word and be 100 percent certain that the word will come off the board. Or if your opponent plays a word that implies that another form of the word, say a past tense, should be in the lexicon but you know it is not, you can challenge your opponent's word with impunity. For example, one of the lists I have memorized contains all eight-letter three-vowel words with two high-point tiles in them. If an opponent were to try RETHAW, I would challenge immediately, since I know that RETHAWED is not on my list.

The major disadvantage of memorization is that it is time consuming. Although it takes an experienced memorizer no longer than five minutes to memorize twenty or so new words, these words must be rehearsed regularly to keep recall from deteriorating. The more new words you memorize, the more memorized words you will have to maintain.

I have memorized 16,000 bingos. Even though 16,000 is a large number, it is less than a third of all seven- and eight-letter words in the OSPD. I learned long ago that I am not capable of memorizing the entire dictionary. The practical consequence of this fact is that I have had to be selective. Except for the unpluralizable three-, four-, and five-letter words, I do not memorize words other than bingos. There are two reasons for this. Shorter words can be remembered through word recognition alone, and shorter words are much more easily anagrammed than bingos. Most of my memorized words are eight-letter bingos rather than sevens. I thus reserve my memorization skills for the words that I might not find over the board had I not memorized them. These include eight-letter bingos containing three or more vowels, plus all seven-letter bingos containing four or more vowels. I do not memorize -S pluralizations of seven-letter bingos unless the pluralization seems strange to me (e.g., MINIMALS). I lose some precision by omitting pluralizations (I once incorrectly played CUNEATES, for example), but this is more than offset by the benefit of not having to memorize many thousands of additional words.

Most players use a straight alphabetical system for storing their memorized words. They arrange the tiles alphabetically on their rack from left to right and then try to recall that portion of their list that most closely corresponds to this alphabetization. A portion of the list comprising all seven-letter bingos arranged in this manner would include the following sequence of words: ABILITY, MISBIAS, ABIOSIS, JABIRUS, KABUKIS. Their alphabetizations are ABIILTY, ABIIMSS, ABIIOSS, ABIJRSU, and ABIKKSU. If you had memorized this list and had ABIIRST on your rack, you would immediately know that you did not have a playable seven-letter bingo, since this combination "falls in the crack" between ABIIOSS and ABIJRSU. My own organizational system is somewhat more involved. My grand list contains sub-lists arranged by how many high-point tiles the words in them contain, and these sub-lists are further broken down according to the number of vowels contained by the words in them. These still lengthy sub-sub-lists are then alphabetized by vowel combinations, and further alphabetized within each vowel combination on the basis of their consonants. To give you an idea of what I am talking about, my one-high-point-letter, four-vowel sub-list begins with the following sequence: ATALAYA, CARAGANA, ANASARCA, ALAMEDA, APANAGE, ALTHAEA, AZALEAS. . . . It ends some 3,400 words later with . . . OUTSHOUT, TUMOROUS, TUBULOUS, UNCTUOUS, and TUMULOUS.

Because of the nature of my lists, I do not arrange tiles alphabetically on my rack. I instead alphabetize the vowels and consonants separately. The vowels are placed to the left, the consonants to the right. I don't leave a gap on my rack between vowels and consonants because I do not want my opponent to know how many of each I have.

Regardless how you organize your lists, you will need some sort of mental filing system to make them manageable. Such a system will enable you to recall specific portions of a large list when you need them. I divide my lists into 200-word groups, and I subdivide each group into ten 20-word units. I learn only one new unit a day, though I may rehearse several hundred previously learned words on the same day. It is vitally important to memorize the sequence of words consisting of the first word in each unit (words #1, #21, #41 . . . #181 of your list), and also the sequence of words consisting of the first word in each group (words #1, #201, #401, and so forth). These guide word lists will greatly shorten the time it takes you to get to the specific portion of the long master list that you need.

HOW TO MEMORIZE. Memorization of so many words is difficult at first, but becomes much easier with practice. There are numerous mnemonic tools at your disposal. Suppose, for example, that you wish to memorize the following sequence of words: RECOOKED, LOCOWEED, COOPERED, DOVECOTE, RECHOOSE, PODOMERE, PEREOPOD, FOVEOLET, and GEOPHONE. These words are from my two-high-point-letter, four-vowel list. The key to remembering them is to find some sort of structure. You may notice, for example, that the first three words end in D, and the second three end in E. You might also categorize them by consonants: the first five contain C, the next two contain D. Another technique is to use tile values to help you memorize: the number 11321 represents the tile values of the initial letter in each of the first five words, for example. Then comes 3342.

Some players like to make up fantastic stories to help them link words together. An example of such a story, as applied to the sequence given above, is:

A starving beggar RECOOKED LOCOWEED in order to survive. In order to get a job, he entered a job retraining program where he learned to be a cooper (COOPERED). He didn't make much money, however, and the only lodging he could afford was a rather unpleasant outdoor flat located right under a DOVECOTE (yecch!). He decided to RECHOOSE his profession to better himself, and became a veterinarian specializing in insect care. His first patient was an arthropod with a broken PODOMERE, and his second was a PEREOPOD with an unsightly FOVEOLET. Upon seeing it, he exclaimed, "Gee. Oh. There's the phone ringing" (GEOPHONE).

Read through this story once or twice, and I think that you will have little problem memorizing the sequence of words embedded within it. The more pictorial and fantastical the story, the easier it is to remember the words. A side benefit is that you will learn the definitions of all sorts of strange words— at least those words that you don't make up definitions for.

If you decide to memorize words, be forewarned that it will take a considerable amount of over-the-board practice before you will be able to apply your labor to actual play. It is one thing to recall words in the peace and quiet of your own home, and quite another to recall them in the middle of a tense tournament game. When I first attempted to use my memorized lists in tournaments, I was unable to recall them at critical moments. Like tile tracking, it was only after considerable tournament experience that I could apply this skill easily and reliably.

ANAGRAMMING. The ability to form words from a seemingly random collection of tiles is of course central to good SCRABBLE play. Knowing that a word is in the OSPD won't help you much if you can't find it over the board. Fortunately, anagramming is a skill that improves with practice. When I first started playing SCRABBLE, I used to test my anagrammatic ability by working on the Jumbles that appear in many daily newspapers. I was initially inept, but now I can routinely find all six six-letter words in the weekend Jumbles puzzle within a total of ten seconds or less. Here are some ways for improving your anagramming ability:

Look for words with prefixes and suffixes.

This is second nature to almost all players. Although the search for these words often proves fruitful, it does entail some risk. Anagramming by prefix and suffix is too easy! It does not tax the player's mind. All too often I have seen players fail to develop true creative anagramming skill because they focus exclusively on prefixes and suffixes. Look for these words, but don't begin and end your search for the best play with them.

Make up combinations of short words and prefixes or suffixes to help you remember real words that are difficult to anagram.

You might, for example, find it useful to remember the word MRIDANGA as DRAMA + ING, KILLDEE as DEL + LIKE, or NUGATORY as OUT + ANGRY. Many players make up lists containing mnemonic rearrangements like these.

Use vocalization as a prompt.

If you have what appears to be a bingo-conducive rack but you cannot find a bingo in it, make up nonsense words from your tiles and say them softly to yourself. If there is in fact a bingo in your rack that you are not unfamiliar with, vocalization of this sort often results in the bingo suddenly popping into your head.

Practice makes better.

The more you test yourself with anagrams, the better you will get at solving them. Joe Edley, a three-time winner of the Nationals, mastered the OSPD almost exclusively by solving anagrams. He uses flash cards, each of which contains ten anagram problems. Joe has gone through all of the bingos in the OSPD many times by solving their anagrams with his flash cards. His training has thus enabled him not only to recognize words in the OSPD, but to anagram them flawlessly as well.

Board resourcefulness

Board resourcefulness refers to the ability to find plays over the board. It is the most important as well as the most creative skill that a player can develop. We shall see in the annotated games section of this book that even among experts, mistakes occur. Such mistakes sometimes result from inadequate vocabulary, poor anagramming skill, or inappropriate strategy. Most frequently, however, they occur because something in the board position is overlooked. Due to time pressure, carelessness, poor visual-spatial ability, or lack of concentration, the player misses the best play.

Board resourcefulness comes from the study of positions. One effective approach is to record the letters of your racks on the score sheet while playing a game, so that it is possible to go back over the game later to see what you missed. Careful postgame analysis, especially if aided by a computer program such as Quackle, almost always reveals many mistakes, and sustained study of this type will sharpen your play over the board. This type of study is time consuming, however, and cannot be rushed. It may take a couple of hours or more of analysis to examine adequately your moves from just one game.

A technique that I sometimes use while playing a game is to take notes on openings created by my opponent or by me. I might write, for instance, "keep H for B6" in a corner of my score sheet to prevent myself from forgetting about this possibility later in the game.

One final tip: board resourcefulness can only be developed fully if you look at the board! Look for opportunities such as those discussed in Chapter 4: openings, hooks, overlaps, inside plays, and word extensions. Too many players spend excessive time with eyes fixated on their tiles. Study the board, and let it guide you to the best play.

Strategic prowess

Most experts acquired their strategic prowess by playing numerous games against, and by consulting with, players who were initially much stronger than they were. There is no substitute for this experience. If you want to develop a good strategic sense, you must see good strategy in action. This book will help you a great deal, but the impact of the principles and ideas presented in it will become real only when they are used against you. When you play an expert, you will feel frustrated when she closes down the exact portion of the board where you were planning to play a bingo. You will feel helpless as she creates an unblockable hook for herself. You will wonder why she always seems to balance her rack while you are stuck with five vowels. In short, you will feel totally outclassed. Once you have experienced these things, the importance of good strategy will become obvious to you. You might have known previously that rack balancing was important, but now you will have acquired the willpower to resist making an inferior play that leaves you with garbage. You will start looking more consciously for plays that set up your remaining tiles or that have defensive merit, rather than going for the play that simply scores a bunch of points. In short, you will begin making plays that make your opponents feel as uncomfortable as you once felt.

Even if you already have a well-developed strategic sense, you should test yourself against good players as part of your pre-tournament preparation. Your strategic skills will be sharpened and you will be more likely to learn a few additional words by playing strong players than by playing weaker ones. Most important, you will be forced to struggle. You will have to exert yourself on every move in order to win. If you can get yourself to adopt a competitive attitude in practice, then you will come close to doing the best that you can in the tournament. If instead, after making a weak move, you say to yourself,

"In a tournament I wouldn't have done that," you may in fact end up doing *exactly* that in a tournament.

Some players avoid playing strong opponents before a tournament because they fear that consistent losing will destroy their self-confidence. This is akin to whistling in the dark. If you are not good enough to win, you might as well know it. If you don't know that you are not good enough, not only will you not try as hard as you should to improve, but you are likely to be very disappointed by your tournament performance. Losing can be good for you, but it feels a whole lot less painful if it occurs before rather than during a tournament.

CHAPTER 7

At the Tournament

This chapter deals with how you should handle yourself at the tournament site in order to both play as well as you possibly can and have an enjoyable experience. The major premise underlying the previous chapter was that pre-tourney study and training contribute greatly to successful tournament results. However, all your preparation will be for naught if you do not look out for yourself at the tournament site. This involves more than maintaining your physical and mental well-being. It requires that you know how to deal with certain situations that may arise during play so that your opponents do not take advantage of you and so that you do not offend other players by exhibiting poor etiquette.

Take care of yourself

Many players enjoy having a good time while attending a tournament. They view tournaments primarily as mini-vacations. There is nothing wrong with this attitude. Tournaments should be enjoyable, even for serious players. Nevertheless, you cannot go hog wild at a tournament and expect to do well. If you eat and drink to excess, don't get enough sleep, and play lots of extra games a day, do not expect to excel in the official competition. In order to do your best, try to maintain your pre-tournament general preparation program: regular exercise, sensible eating, plenty of rest and relaxation, and abstinence from substances that cloud your judgment and concentration.

There are some precautions you can take that will help you conserve your energy. First, spend as little time as possible in the tournament area between games. There is usually about a ten-minute interlude between the end of a round and the beginning of the following round. Use this time to go back to your room or to go someplace quiet where you can relax for a short while. If you hang around the playing room, you may get caught up in an animated conversation about how you and everyone else fared in the previous round. Don't expend a great deal of energy bemoaning your fate or describing how brilliantly you played.

Pig out at dinner, if you must, not at meals preceding tournament play. Lunch can be especially dangerous, as after three or four hard games in the morning you are likely to be very hungry. If you eat too much, your body's need to digest the food is likely to make you somnolent for a while.

If you have a little extra time during the lunch break, go back to your room and take a shower. It will refresh you and help you play well in the afternoon.

Finally, don't study too much over the days of the tournament. I find such study to be more harmful than helpful. It reduces your confidence by exposing you to many words that you may not be able to absorb in a short period of time, and if you in fact already know them, then study is of little value anyway. Studying during a tournament always makes me feel somewhat frantic, and I don't believe it has ever helped me. However, I cannot make a blanket condemnation of cramming, since I know a few experts who say that they find this type of study beneficial, even relaxing.

Table manners

The nature of SCRABBLE tournament play is such that it is easy to upset or distract your opponent. If you are an inexperienced tournament player, you may not even realize that your opponent is taking unfair advantage of you by engaging in such behavior. You may also unknowingly irritate your opponent. For these reasons, it is important to know something about proper SCRABBLE etiquette.

Good etiquette

Good etiquette consists of playing quietly, presenting a pleasant demeanor, and making no attempt whatsoever to distract the opponent. It does not preclude a few allowable deceptions, however. You are not breaching good etiquette if you actively but quietly shuffle the tiles on your rack to give your opponent the false impression that your tiles are very promising. Your opponent might make a defensive play as a result, rather than the higher-scoring play she was intending. It also is allowable to stare intently at part of the board so that your opponent might think, again erroneously, that you plan to play there on your next move. You should feel free to time your plays in potential challenge situations. If you intend to play a word that you know is acceptable but you think might be challenged, you might hesitate before making the play so as to induce your opponent to think you are unsure about the word's acceptability. If you play a phony, on the other hand, you might play it immediately and with confidence so that your opponent will get the impression that you are certain the word in question is acceptable.

Bad etiquette

Bad etiquette mainly consists of talking during the game other than for the purposes of announcing the number of points scored for a play, rectifying scoring discrepancies between you and your opponent, informing him of a decision to exchange tiles or to pass, and challenging. The nontechnical name for such chatter is coffeehousing. Your opponent may be struggling to recall words from a memorized word list, trying to deal with the strategic implications of competing moves, or attempting to anagram an eight-letter bingo. If you say something as innocuous as "My, what a nice day. Too bad we are cooped up in here," you might break his concentration. He will be perfectly justified in telling you to be quiet.

Other types of comments seem more intentionally designed to rile the opposing player. Among the most common are those intended to mislead about the tiles in a player's rack: "I just can't seem to pick any decent tiles today." "What junk!" or "Oh, wow, finally something good." Ignore comments like these. Never believe your opponent, and never believe that the opposite of what your opponent says is true either. Make your play on what you know, not what your opponent tells you.

Other kinds of remarks may be intended to deceive you into erroneously challenging or refraining from challenging. I wish I had a dollar for every instance in which an opponent placed a word on the board and then said, "I'm not really sure whether this is good." The unspoken message behind such a remark is *if you decide to challenge and you lose the challenge, you really aren't so dumb, because even I don't know if the word is good. So go ahead and challenge.* Experience has shown me that plays prefaced by expressions of hesitancy are almost always acceptable.

Another way of saying "I'm not sure if this word is good" is to place a word on the board and ask the opponent if it is acceptable. The player may be genuinely unsure if her word is allowable. And it would, therefore, be very helpful for her to know if you intend to challenge the word, should she play it! Don't answer her question. Don't even say that you don't know if the word is good, since any indication of uncertainty on your part may be taken as a signal that you will not challenge. Say something like, "Sorry, I won't answer that now," which not only makes the point but also implies that you do know the answer. I must admit, however, that I am on occasion sorely tempted to say, "Yes, of course it's okay," when I know that it isn't, and then challenge the word after my opponent presses her clock button.

Do not pronounce the words you play. Do not talk to yourself. Do not bemoan your bad luck or your opponent's good luck, and don't get sarcastic and compliment your opponent for a pedestrian play, by saying, "Nice play," after she has played away the Z and two other tiles for 45 points. On the other hand, if your opponent plays something brilliant go ahead and compliment her—briefly, and on your clock time.

There are a few nonverbal ways of exhibiting bad etiquette. Some players develop coughing fits that mysteriously vanish when it is their turn to play but return when it is their opponent's turn. Others squirm in their seats a great deal. Some are experts in making faces of despair, joy, horror, and so forth. Others stare at you more than they look at their own racks. Still others shuffle their tiles as loudly as possible. I once played against an opponent who, after picking his tiles, kept the bag on his side of the table, as far away from me as possible. Also annoying is the habit some players have of moving the board from its position in the middle of the table closer to them, or so far from them that their opponents have no room on the table for their racks. Finally, a few players seem to obtain great delight from twirling around the board of a deluxe set immediately after their opponent has made a play, causing the board to bump into their opponent's rack, spilling their opponent's tiles onto the floor.

Cheating

There are numerous ways to cheat at SCRABBLE, including looking into the bag, using word lists during play, picking excess tiles and storing some of them in a pocket for future play, purposely adding the score incorrectly to one's advantage, banking points (purposefully underscoring oneself in order to win the game on a recount), and so forth. It is difficult to deal with cheating, since it is almost impossible to catch a cheater red-handed. No one wants to falsely accuse someone of cheating.

If you suspect your opponent of cheating, you are in a bind. You can attempt to blot the thought from your mind and focus on playing well, or you can watch your opponent like a hawk, in which case your own play may suffer. It's a very difficult situation, and I don't really know which choice you should make.

Fortunately, cheating at this game is a rare phenomenon. There have been some recent cases of cheaters being caught, however. The minimum ban is getting tossed out of a tournament. The maximum penalty meted out so far: a four-year ban on playing in SCRABBLE clubs and tournaments.

Board orientation

According to the rules, you are entitled to turn the board to any position you prefer when it is your turn to play. Some players, however, find it unsettling if the board is turned during play. They may choose to play upside down so that turning the board is not necessary, or they may ask you to play sideways. Unless you have a lot of experience playing sideways, don't accede to this request and don't feel guilty about your refusal. Your opponent may think you are being spiteful, but all you are doing is refusing to accept a handicap.

If you are not used to playing directly opposite your opponent, with the board either right side up or upside down, I would suggest that you get used to it by playing pre-tourney practice games. I would also suggest that you get into the habit of playing right side up rather than upside down. There are a number of experts who do in fact play upside down, and they claim that they are at least as adept with this orientation as they would be if they played right side up. My experience is that they have a slightly higher likelihood of playing two-letter words backward (e.g., IH instead of HI; IX instead of XI) than do players who play right side up.

I know two players who always play upside down. I wonder what they do when they play each other.

Time pressure

Your success in tournament play will be affected considerably by how you handle time pressure. It is vitally important that you use your time as effectively as possible. If you play too quickly, you will make more mistakes than if you play a bit more deliberately. If you play too slowly, the consequences are likely to be substantial. You may overstep the time limit and be penalized, or the necessity for you to play quickly in the endgame to keep from going over the limit may cause you to blunder. Try to pace yourself so that you have about five to ten minutes on your clock when there are fewer than seven tiles in the bag. Learn to do this by playing numerous pre-tournament practice games using the clock.

Many players squander time early in the game. The most common instance is to spend five or six minutes looking for bingos that "should" be there. Don't invest such a large chunk of time for this purpose. If you cannot find a bingo within three minutes, it is extremely unlikely that you will find one within six.

Don't take a rest when it is your opponent's turn to play. You can save valuable minutes by making contingency plans during this time. Think about what you might do if your opponent plays in one sector of the board versus what you might do should she play elsewhere. If your opponent is using up a lot of time by playing slowly, you should be prepared to play even more quickly. By forcing her to think more or less exclusively on her own time, your quick play may exacerbate her time trouble.

On the other hand, don't be intimidated by an opponent who plays at lightning speed. It is very easy to get caught up in the rhythm of quick play and to play faster than you should. Opponents who play quickly are experts at it. If you allow such an opponent to dictate the pace of the game, he is likely to play closer to his potential than you will to yours. The fast player may not play as well as he would if he took more time, but he usually plays better rapidly than his opponents play rapidly. I deal with what seems like excessively fast play by my opponent by letting at least a minute of time go by on my clock before moving, even if I know what I am going to do. Why rush? Maybe your opponent is dying to use the washroom. I vividly remember a game I played several years ago in which my opponent achieved a lead of 150 points after only five minutes of play. I then took some deep breaths to calm myself, and deliberately slowed my play drastically. My opponent seemed to lose interest in the game, and I won it by a few points.

Poise

One of the dominant tournament SCRABBLE players of the mid-1970s was Mike Senkiewicz. I played him only once, in my very first tournament. I lost the game, but what impressed me more than his play was his poise. He was remarkably still throughout the game. His eyes were focused entirely upon his rack or the board, and he seemed hardly to notice me. Both his board etiquette and his ability to concentrate were exemplary.

In contrast to this behavior, I think of my own performance at the 1980 Canadian Regional Qualifier. This was a high-stakes tournament, as the top four finishers from a field of thirty-two players would qualify for an all-expense-paid trip to the Nationals to be held in Santa Monica the following month. I won the first seven games of the ten-game tournament and then fell apart. I lost the next two games, and I would have failed to qualify had I lost my last game by more than 45 points.

My opponent in the final game was Reg Lever. Reg had been one of the finest players in Great Britain before he emigrated to Canada, but he was legally blind at the time of this tournament. A special high-intensity lamp was placed next to the playing table to help him. Was I calm and collected, as Mike Senkiewicz had been against me? Not on your life. I was thinking about how awful it would be if I lost this critical game to a legally blind person and failed to qualify for the Nationals. I relaxed a bit after achieving a 140-point lead, but Reg stormed back with two bingos and a 42-point play. When all the tiles had been taken from the bag, he had a 5-point lead, the remaining blank, and it was his turn. I may not have looked like a mess, but that is how I felt inside. I was unable to concentrate at all. I should have been thinking about the game situation. Instead, I was contemplating giving up tournament play forever. I felt helpless, as if my loss were preordained. I had played miserably over the preceding five or six turns and was about to be punished for doing so. And then I got very lucky, for it was at this moment that Reg decided to play a phony, GILA. The challenge killed his winning chances, and my nightmare was over. Luck won out over panic.

Although I have experienced similar panicky moments in tournament play since my game against Reg, I have learned how to control myself a bit better. The key to accomplishing this is to recognize and then combat the first symptoms of the problem. These symptoms include the standard physical indicators of anxiety, such as sweaty or clammy hands, difficulty in fine motor coordination, dryness of the throat, shortness of breath, and the disruption of concentration. In SCRABBLE, panic-stricken players usually play either overcautiously or impulsively. Overcautious play reflects "SCRABBLE paranoia," the unfounded belief that the opponent must have great tiles. Impulsivity, on the other hand, occurs because the afflicted player feels very uncomfortable and wants to end the game quickly. Too much caution is bad, but impulsive play can be even worse.

You should always try to play deliberately rather than impulsively. If you find a so-so play quickly, look for a better one. If you locate a good one, use a little more time to see if you can find a very good one.

The example on the next page comes from a club game that I played against a very fine player. She had in fact beaten me in each of the previous three games we had played. This particular game was the last of the session. We were both tired, and one of the reasons tiredness is so detrimental to good play is that, like anxiety, it fosters impulsive play. One just doesn't want to be bothered to look.

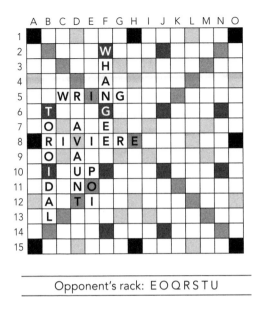

Opponent's rack: E O Q R S T U

My opponent played TORQUES (I2, 79) immediately after I had made my previous play, which was TOROIDAL. Hers was a knee-jerk reaction play: she had planned it beforehand, and she didn't even look to see if my play had altered the board in a way that might have affected her choice. About ten seconds afterward, she groaned horribly. She had noticed that TORQUES could have instead been played at A1 for 132 points! Too bad for her that she didn't take those few extra seconds before making her play.

The most comical form of blunder occurs when a player spends two or three minutes trying to decide between two possible plays and then spots another play that he hadn't considered before. He makes this third play immediately, and soon afterward rues his action.

There are a number of things you can do to develop good over-the-board poise. First, relax. Slow down a little. Second, be sensitive to changes in your composure. If you know that you are falling apart, you may be more capable of limiting the damage than if you are unaware of what is happening to you. You might then make a conscious effort to restrain yourself from playing too hastily. Third, try not to allow a loss to affect your future play. It is very common for players to lose in streaks. This happens because once poise is lost it is hard to regain later in the same day. If you have blundered horribly, you may find it difficult to blot out that blunder after the game is over. Or you may think that because you played poorly earlier in the day, there is nothing to prevent you from playing poorly throughout the tournament.

Good poise can be developed from experience in tournament play. I mention this to cushion you from being disappointed if you do not do as well in your first few tournaments as you feel you should. The more time you invest in pre-tournament study and training, the greater will be the psychological burden you place on yourself to play well. You may think that you deserve to place well. For a few fortunate people this is in fact what happens, but most of us have to stumble through our first several competitions before we really know what is happening. Don't resent it if players whom you know to be weaker than you place higher than you do. This will happen less frequently with greater tournament experience.

CHAPTER 8

Annotated Games

The eight annotated games included in this section were all played by experts. I have chosen them on the basis of their high quality. All were played in tournaments and were therefore timed. Perfectly played SCRABBLE games are rare, however, and mistakes in complicated positions or in the endgame occurred with some frequency. Still, there were some remarkably good plays.

In order to benefit as much as possible from the games, I suggest that you get out your SCRABBLE set and play along. Or, you can use a blank board diagram and a pencil. For each move, cover up both the portion of the page showing the player's move and my commentary below it. Then allow yourself two minutes to find your best play. Write down the play, and then study the situation for a few more minutes. In many instances you will discover plays that are better than your original ones. This exercise will give you a feeling for how difficult it is to make the best play under time pressure. Also, track tiles and use the information gained from your tile tracking to help you choose your plays.

After you have thoroughly examined a position, take a look at the move that was played and at my commentary. Then add it to the board and proceed onward to the next move. This approach will force you to *participate*. You will learn many new words and you will improve your strategic sense from studying my commentary, but it is the active searching for the best play that will most sharpen your game.

Unlike most of the situations presented earlier in the chapters devoted to strategy, many of the positions in these annotated games have no clear-cut solutions. In such cases I have tried to show how competing moves that are about equally good attempt to fulfill the same priorities, or how they may differ in terms of their strengths and weaknesses.

I have supplemented my commentary with occasional simulations from Quackle. Results for each iteration are calculated after each player has made two moves, and they are based on a minimum of two thousand such iterations. In many but not nearly all cases, Quackle simulations provide very accurate indications of the strengths of competing plays.

Game #1: Almost Perfect

Carl Johnson vs. Dave Wiegand
Oregon Tile Tournament, May 2009

This was an exciting ultra-high-quality game, played by two of the best. One of the two players, Dave Wiegand, made optimal moves on all of his plays.

....

1. Carl Johnson: **C K L N R T U**
    CLUNK (8H, 32, 32)

    An obvious move: an optimal score combined with the optimal leave.
    Fear of the -ERS, -IER, -ING extensions does not warrant sacrificing
    4 points by playing CLUNK at 8D.

    Dave Wiegand: **I I N O R V Z**
    VIRION (K3, 18, 18)

    Another obvious play (if you know the word).

....

2. Carl Johnson: **B C E M O R T**
    MOB (J4, 29, 61)

    So far, so good. CERT is a nice rack leave.

    Dave Wiegand: **A A D E N S Z**
    CADENZAS (H8, 113, 131)

    A huge, beautiful play!

....

3. Carl Johnson: **A C E G O R T**
    ESCARGOT (15G, 63, 124)

    Having to play a word that ends one square before a triple word score
    is scary, to say the least. This is Carl's only bingo, however, and so he
    has to play it.

    Dave Wiegand: **E I P R T W Y**
    CLUNKIER (8H, 42, 173)

    This nice extension outscores the next-highest-scoring plays by 11 points
    (TWYER, M6; YIPE, G9) and is slightly better than YEW (14M, 27)
    and WYE (M7, 29).

4. **Carl Johnson: F G I N N R T**

RIFTING (M7, 32, 156)

Maximum points, decent leave: an easy choice.

Dave Wiegand: E E O P T W Y

YOWE (G9, 33, 206)

Another play that is clearly better than anything else. So far, both players are coasting along and playing perfectly. They have not had to make any difficult decisions.

5. **Carl Johnson: E N N O R X ☐**

EXONS (O11, 90, 246)

Ouch!

Dave Wiegand: A A E P S T V

PAT (F10, 32, 238)

VAV (3K, 18) yields the best leave, AEPST, but on this rather closed board the sacrifice of 14 points isn't worth it. Other plays at F10 (PA and PATE) are almost as good as PAT.

6. **Carl Johnson: A E E L N R ☐**

LARCENER (O1, 71, 317)

A touch sloppy. Better in the same location are both NEARLIER and ENLARGER (74 points each). I prefer ENLARGER, as NEARLIER places vowels adjacent to both a double word score and a triple letter score.

Dave Wiegand: A D E E H S V

HAVE (13C, 26, 264)

This play sets up the S for 13B. HEAVE (13B, 28) scores 2 more points and also sets up the S, this time on a triple word score row. However, it is important to keep an E. The leave of DES is much better than the leave of DS.

7.   Carl Johnson: E I I S T U U

Exchange IUU (0, 317)

> *UKE (L7, 15) is cute, but it is a play without a future. An exchange of*
> *tiles is necessary, and Carl makes the right one by holding on to EIST.*
> *Keeping only EST is almost as good, however.*

Dave Wiegand: A D E I L S Y

DIALYSE (B8, 87, 351)

> *Nice.*

....

8.   Carl Johnson: E H I P R S T

TRIPHASE (D8, 80, 397)

> *Beautiful.*

Dave Wiegand: A D F I O T T

DITTO (A4, 33, 384)

> *This play scores and simulates as well as FIDO (A5, 33), but I like*
> *it better. Dave might play FA (14J, 28) next turn, if there is nothing*
> *better.*

9. **Carl Johnson: E I M N O S U**

Unseen tiles: A A B D E F G I J L O Q U U W

MU (L11, 16, 413)

> *I suspect that Carl made this move in order to prevent Dave from playing a possible QI (L11). Regardless, this was not the right play. If he had retained an A for K11, this might be a good play, but it really doesn't do much for him otherwise.*
>
> *Quackle recommends OUT (N13, 14), which retains a great EIMNS leave. I prefer Quackle's second choice, however: UN (14N, 8). Why? Because if Carl picks one of the five unseen vowels from the bag, he might be able to play a bingo next turn at 4A (DAIMONES or DOMAINES, DEMONISE, DOMINIES, DOMINOES).*
>
> *Another way to go would be to play MEN or ME at L4, scoring well and taking out a potentially high-scoring line. After MEN, Carl would have a 45-point lead. Dave would probably need a bingo to beat him.*

Dave Wiegand: A E F G I J W

Unseen tiles: A B D E I L N O O Q S U U

JAG (K10, 36, 420)

> *Dave takes advantage of the new line created by Carl's last play.*

10. **Carl Johnson: A E I N O O S**

Unseen tiles: B D E F I L Q U U W

ZOOS (13H, 26, 439)

> *Carl breaks one of the cardinal rules of SCRABBLE strategy— he empties the bag when he need not do so. Fortunately for him, Dave has such awkward tiles that knowledge of Carl's complete rack will not be of much help. Better plays would have been OOT (N13, 14), OAK (L6, 15), and JATO (10K, 18).*

Dave Wiegand: D E F I Q U W

Carl's rack (all of the unseen tiles): A B E I L N U

QUA (2M, 24, 444)

Leaving himself the out play of WIFED (B1, 30), but knowing that Carl will block it. Had Dave played WIFED first, Carl would win by first blocking QUA (2M) with VILER (3K, 16). Then after Dave's QI (2A), Carl could play out with BUNA (E5, 14) for a 471–461 victory.

....

11. Carl Johnson: A B E I L N U
DULIA (4A, 12, 451)

> *Beautiful play, unforeseen even by Quackle! Dave can neither play out nor prevent Carl from playing out first. Another winning combination for Carl would have been TUNABLE (6A, 13) followed by QI (M2, 22).*

Dave Wiegand: D E F I W
WIFE (5E, 30, 474)

....

12. Carl Johnson: B E N
BEN (L4, 32, 483)

> *+4 for the D on Dave's rack: 487*

Final score: Carl Johnson 487, Dave Wiegand 474.

Game #2: Clash of the Titans

Brian Cappelletto vs. Adam Logan
Can-Am Challenge, 2008

Brian Cappelletto and Adam Logan have each won National and World Championships. They are perennially at the top of the ratings list, and undoubtedly are among the top three or four players in North America.

....

1. **Brian Cappelletto: A C E G I S ☐**
   CEASI<u>N</u>G (8D, 74, 74)

   The other bingos are CAGIES<u>T</u> and I<u>N</u>CAGES. Brian's play is best, as it doesn't expose any double letter scores to vowels.

   Adam Logan: A A E E E V W (0, 0)
   Exchange AAEEVW

   Surely this is not the right play. WAE (7E) scores 17 points, has some defensive merit, and its AEEV leave is not awful. Or WEAVES (G3, 17) gets rids of both the V and the W. It creates a potentially dangerous play for Brian from H1, but the likelihood of Brian scoring an additional 17 points here, versus what he might get if Adam exchanges, is low. Think of it this way: Adam has sacrificed 17 points for the privilege of picking to an E rather than picking to AE.

....

2. **Brian Cappelletto: D G K O T T V**
   VOTED (E6, 18, 92)

   By far the best play. GAVOT (F7, 11), VODKA (F4, 17), and TOKED (E5, 20) all simulate about 5 points worse than VOTED, because they either have worse leaves than VOTED or don't score as well.

   Adam Logan: A E E F H R ☐
   FOREHEA<u>D</u> (6D, 67, 67)

   Nice play.

3.   Brian Cappelletto: E G K N S T V

KEG (5J, 24, 116)

> *There are four plays here that are about equally good: VEST (L4, 28) or*
> *VETS (L3, 28), KEGS (G5, 11), and Brian's play of KEG. I am partial*
> *to VETS, as it is slightly more defensive than VEST and takes an early*
> *53-point lead on a fairly quiet board.*

Adam Logan: A A J N O Y Z

ZANY (4K, 49, 116)

> *Nothing else is close to this move.*

4.   Brian Cappelletto: E M N S T V W

SWEVENS (G2, 18, 134)

> *Brian was a little too anxious to dispose of both the V and the W.*
> *A much better play is MEWS (G5, 13), retaining the S and ENTV*
> *to go with it. The leave of MT after SWEVENS is worth 0, whereas*
> *VENTS has a valuation of 7.5.*

Adam Logan: A E I O O J S

JIAO (3L, 42, 158)

> *This play nicely dispenses with a lot of vowels along with the J.*

5.   Brian Cappelletto: A E L M O T T

TEAM (F1, 21, 155)

> *TOTEMS (2B, 28) scores highest here, plus its AL leave is no worse*
> *than the LOT leave after Brian's TEAM. ALT (2M, 23) is a reasonable*
> *alternative, but TOTEMS is better.*

	A	B	C	D	E	F	G	H	I	J	K	L	M	N	O
1						T									
2						E	S								
3						A	W					J	I	A	O
4						M	E				Z	A	N	Y	
5					V		V		K	E	G				
6			F	O	R	E	H	E	A	D					
7				T		N									
8				C	E	A	S	I	N	G					
9				D											
10															
11															
12															
13															
14															
15															

Adam Logan: B E E O N P S

COPEN (D8, 21, 179)

> Adam misses a great chance for a setup: PAY (N2, 16). He holds the last
> S, and both blanks are gone, so PAY holds no risk. Moreover, there is no
> easy way for Brian to block a play along the top row. COPEN is second
> best and it simulates a full 9 points behind PAY.

....

6. **Brian Cappelletto:** O D D L P Q T

TODDLES (2A, 18, 173)

> With all four U's unseen, it makes little sense to trade in the Q.
> TODDLES offers the best chance of picking a U, though placing a T
> in the triple column is somewhat dangerous. POD (C9, 25) is certainly
> a viable alternative, as is DOLT (E11, 18). DOLT isn't particularly
> dangerous, considering that the blanks and three S's are gone, and it
> gives Brian an extra shot at picking a U in comparison to POD. That
> probably doesn't compensate for the 7-point difference.

Adam Logan: B B E O R S X

BOX (C11, 30, 209)

> *The right play. Quackle has OXO (O1) simulating within a point of*
> *BOX, but with the possibility of setting up an unblockable hook up there*
> *later with HAY, PAY, or WAY, it is best not to take the spot.*

---

7. **Brian Cappelletto: E I U U P Q T**

QUAY (N1, 32, 205)

> *Quackle comes up with a play that I bet few humans would have*
> *thought of: PTUI (A1, 21). This move simulates 4.5 points higher than*
> *Brian's obvious QUAY. Why?*
>
> > *First, there are six I's unseen. Even though Brian retains an I, the*
> > *likelihood is very high that Adam will have QI (1N, 33) as a possibility.*
> > *Second, PTUI takes away the only realistic spot for a bingo on this*
> > *board. Third, and possibly most pivotal, is that the leave of EIPTU*
> > *after QUAY is much weaker than EQTU after PTUI: −6.7 versus*
> > *+9.9!*

Adam Logan: B E I N R S U

TRIBUNES (A2, 83, 292)

> *Or TURBINES in the same spot.*

---

8. **Brian Cappelletto: E F I L P T U**

QI (1N, 33, 238)

> *Might as well take the spot now, rather than leave it for Adam. Other*
> *plays such as PULI (B6, 28), PUL (B6, 25), and FEU (B12, 27) are*
> *weaker.*

Adam Logan: D E H I M R S

DIMER (B4, 35, 327)

> *With three E's and three R's still unseen and the board fairly closed for*
> *bingos, it makes a lot of sense for Adam to take the extra 6 points with*
> *DIMER, as opposed to just playing DIM.*

....

9.   **Brian Cappelletto: E F I L P T U**
LEPT (E11, 25, 263)

> *Brian is in dire straits here. In an even game, FEU (B12, 27) would be best. Down 89, however, it is better to open the board a bit with BEFIT (11C, 20). Incidentally, the FIU leave after LEPT is truly awful. Better would have been LEFT in the same spot, even though it takes an S. This is no time for defense.*
>
> *An extreme long shot of a play is PEON (12A, 9). The idea is to get lucky and pick, over the next turn or two, the remaining unseen U and one of the four A's for BEAUTIFUL (11C, 106).*

Adam Logan: I C H L N R S
TIC (14E, 7, 334)

> *I can't say that I am a big fan of this play. True, it blocks three bingo lines, but at the cost of scoring few points and of leaving a rack with five consonants on it. I would not play THIRL (14E, 16), Quackle's recommendation, because of possible bingo plays parallel and above it. But I do like THIRLS (14E, 19), which eliminates almost all possible bingos, for the time being at least.*

10. **Brian Cappelletto: A E F I I I U**

Exchange AFIIU (0, 263)

> *A truly awful rack. Unfortunately, the exchange will not help very much.*

Adam Logan: A H L N R R S

HARL (B12, 30, 364)

> *A no-brainer.*

---

11. **Brian Cappelletto: E I O O T T W**

WOE (A13, 39, 302)

> *Another no-brainer. However, Brian's chances of winning this game are virtually over.*

Adam Logan: A G L N R R S

RAIL (F12, 16, 380)

> *Good play, as it holds back the S for JAGS (L3). Or if Brian opens the board and Adam picks a couple of vowels, Adam might be able to play a bingo.*

---

12. **Brian Cappelletto: A I I I O T T**

Unseen tiles: A E F G N N O R S U U Y

ADIT (D1, 12, 314)

> *The best move, but holding out no hope for victory.*

Adam Logan: A F G N R S U

Unseen tiles: E I I N O O T U Y

JAGS (L3, 26, 406)

> *Scores best and keeps one in the bag. Other good plays are FUSE (I3, 20), AG (H3, 19), and FA (9H, 13).*

---

13. **Brian Cappelletto: E I I O U T Y**

Unseen tiles: A F G N N O R U

GUY (J8, 15, 329)

Adam Logan: A F G N O R U

Cappelletto's rack: E I I N O T

OURANG (K10, 19, 425)

> *It is better to play ELF (15A, 6) first, threatening OURANG and not allowing Brian to have the 24 points he got on his next turn.*

....

14. Brian Cappelletto: E I I N O T

IGNITE (15J, 24, 353)

Adam Logan: F

IF (H8, 5, 430)

> *ELF (15A) is a point better. But it doesn't matter.*
> *+2 for the O on Brian's rack: 432*

Final score: Adam Logan 432, Brian Cappelletto 353.

Game #3: Squeaker #1

Evan Berofsky vs. Jason Katz-Brown
Can-Am Challenge, 2006

An interesting game played by two young experts. The win remains in doubt almost until the end.

....

1.   **Evan Berofsky: A E I O U V Y**

YOU (8G, 12, 12)

> *The best play, and about 3 points better than the best exchange, which is to keep the E only.*

Jason Katz-Brown: A E E H O T Z

ZOEAE (9C, 31, 31)

> *EH (9H, 20) is the play here. Although it sacrifices 11 points versus Jason's play of ZOEAE, it more than makes them up by giving Evan little to play with, and by retaining a superior leave.*

....

2.   **Evan Berofsky: A A A E I N V**

AVIAN (7D, 18, 30)

> *At least as good as VAIN (10B, 30), which retains a horrible leave, and AVA (10A, 25), which places an A in a triple word square column.*

Jason Katz-Brown: A A F H I T U

FAITH (10B, 55, 86)

> *A sharp four-way overlap play.*

....

3.   **Evan Berofsky: A C E I L O R**

LORICAE (J6, 74, 104)

> *His other 74-point bingos were CARIOLE (J6) and COALIER (J2). LORICAE is best, as it doesn't take an S plural, which CARIOLE does. COALIER offers the opponent more to play with than the other two plays, doesn't interfere with row 11, and allows counterplay down column K and across four rows.*

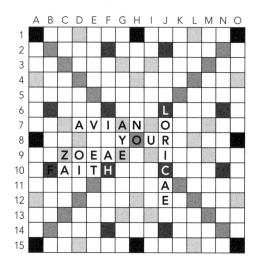

Jason Katz-Brown: A D D N U V X

VAV (E5, 18, 104)

Wonderful play! Jason sets up his X at 6F.

....

4. Evan Berofsky: A B E E E H N

    HAEN (11E, 32, 136)

    Jason's previous play indicates that he either holds the X or is fishing for a bingo. The likelihood is that he has the X. Otherwise he could have played AVA (11J). Although HAEN is the top simulating play, AAH (6D, 29), is the best play here because of Jason's not insignificant threat.

    Jason Katz-Brown: D D N P S U X

    PAX (6D, 57, 161)

....

5. Evan Berofsky: A B B D E E U

    FUBBED (B10, 28, 164)

    Best by a mile over CUBEB, CUBED, and CUBE (10J) and over BEDAUB (12I, 22).

    Jason Katz-Brown: D D F N S S U

    DEFUND (12I, 22, 183)

Another optimal play. Its only competitor is DEFUNDS (12I, 26), but it makes much more sense to play the odds and hope for a play down column O before Evan can get there.

---

6. **Evan Berofsky: A E E I J S W**

JADES (N10, 58, 222)

This is not exactly what Jason was hoping for!

Jason Katz-Brown: G P R S S T T

PIGS (9I, 17, 200)

TUG (11A, 17) is best here. Its five-consonant leave, PRSST, is not as bad as it looks. Also worth consideration is PST (K7, 19).

---

7. **Evan Berofsky: E E I N R W ☐**

W<u>I</u>NERIES (L2, 72, 294)

This move is about as good as the other bingos of REWI<u>D</u>ENS and WI<u>D</u>ENERS (L2, 72), and W<u>H</u>EREIN (K1, 72). Quackle likes ZANIER (C9, 46) just as much as the bingos, but I wouldn't recommend it. The leave of EW ☐ does not guarantee a bingo next turn, and ZANIER closes down a good portion of the board, which is not the thing to do when holding a blank.

Jason Katz-Brown: G O O R S T T

GROTTOS (O5, 85, 285)

Right back in the game! It is amusing that GROTTOS isn't even Jason's best play—DOGTROTS (15B, 86) is.

---

8. **Evan Berofsky: I L L N N Q R**

QUILL (L11, 15, 309)

NNR is not a great leave, but with fifteen consonants and thirteen vowels unseen, chances are good that Evan will pick up a couple of vowels to make life easier on his next play.

Jason Katz-Brown: D E I L M O R

DERMOID (15B, 36, 321)

An easy choice. Not only is it the highest-scoring play, it also uses up the most tiles. With the game coming to a close and a blank still unseen, this is an important factor.

....

9. Evan Berofsky: **G I N N R W Y**
    WINGY (3K, 22, 331)

    A mistake, for the same reasons that Jason's last play was best: other plays use more tiles and score more points. The choices are between WIRING, WINING, and WRYING (31, 26 points for the first two, 32 for the last). There are some great spots for the Y on this board, so I would keep it and go with WIRING or WINING. Quackle rates the three moves about the same.

    Jason Katz-Brown: **E E L T T U** ☐
    Unseen tiles: **A C E I I I K M N O O R R S T**
    UT (14E, 12, 333)

    Played with an eye on the unseen M, which might do a lot of damage at 14F. Nevertheless, BLUET, BUTTE, and BUTLE (13B, 14) accomplish the same thing while scoring 2 more points and taking out a couple of double word scores.

....

10. Evan Berofsky: **E I I I M N R**
    Unseen tiles: **A C E E K L O O R S T T** ☐
    BRIM (13B, 23, 354)

    Evan draws the three-eyed monster, a most unfortunate turn of events. He tries to tough it out by taking the highest score and hoping for the best. Plays down column I (MIRE, IMINE, etc.) seem very dangerous, given the nice collection of unseen tiles.

    Jason Katz-Brown: **E E L O T T** ☐
    Unseen tiles: **A C E I I K N O R S**
    LEY (O1, 18, 351)

    Jason keeps it close while depriving Evan of a possible 30-point play (KAY or KEY at O1). TOY in the same spot might have been better, but it is very hard to tell for sure. A very complicated pre-endgame.

. . . .

11. **Evan Berofsky: A C E I I K N**

Unseen tiles: E O O R S T T ☐

KINA (I3, 15, 369)

> *The mistake that costs him the game. The unseen tiles guarantee Jason a*
> *big play down column K. Evan must block it and then hope for the best.*
> *There are thus two possibilities: WIN (K3, 18) and CAW (2J, 19). As it*
> *turned out, both would have won the game for Evan, but WIN would*
> *have been the easier move to think through in time pressure. Evan's*
> *leave would have been ACEKI plus one of E, O, R, S, or T (assuming*
> *that Jason holds the blank). Jason's highest-scoring play down column*
> *J (attaching an S to WINGY) would have scored 21 points, tying the*
> *game. But then Evan would have had either a big play along row 1*
> *arising from Jason's play, or he would have had ICK (14H, 22)—more*
> *than enough to win, no matter what letters Jason had left on his rack.*

Jason Katz-Brown: E O O R T T ☐

TOWER (K1, 27, 378)

> *The winning play.*

12. Evan Berofsky: C E I S

    SIC (O13, 19, 388)

    Jason Katz-Brown: O T ☐

    TROT (1H, 9, 387)

    Better was DOTS̲ (I12, 16), but only if he was 100 percent positive that
    DERMOIDS was acceptable.

    +2 for the E on Evan's rack: 389

Final score: Jason Katz-Brown 389, Evan Berofsky 388.

Game #4: Robin's Choice

John Luebkemann vs. Robin Pollock-Daniel
Can-Am Challenge, 2006

This beautifully played game between two longtime and distinguished experts comes down to one play: exchange tiles and pray for the best, or grab a small lead and try to defend it with mediocre tiles?

....

1. John Luebkemann: **A A I O P R R**
    APORIA (8C, 22, 22)
    > *Good play: maximum points, a leave no worse than after any other play.*
    Robin Pollock-Daniel: A E O Q T Y ☐
    QAT (7G, 46, 46)

....

2. John Luebkemann: **E E F R R U Z**
    FEZ (7A, 46, 68)
    Robin Pollock-Daniel: D E H O M Y ☐
    HOME<u>B</u>ODY (E7, 82, 128)
    > *A terrific find. It's the only bingo, and it makes little difference if it is played here or at E3.*

....

3. John Luebkemann: **E L L N R R U**
    FULLER (A7, 30, 98)
    > *Nothing competes with this play. The leave after FURLER, LN, is certainly weaker than the NR leave after FULLER is played.*
    Robin Pollock-Daniel: A I I N T U V
    UNITIVE (B1, 36, 164)
    > *Another clear choice. SCRABBLE is an easy game, right?*

....

4. John Luebkemann: **B E I N O R T**
    NOB (A1, 27, 125)
    > *Quackle rates this play about 2 points worse than BO (D12, 19) and*

BIO (D12, 26). Down by 66, I would be tempted to play BO and hope for a quick equalizing bingo next turn. The simulation indicates that Robin will average 3 more points on her next turn following BO or BIO, as opposed to NOB. On the other hand, John averages a bingo 61 percent of the time after playing BO. That declines to 42 percent after BIO and 37 percent after NOB. Yes, BO looks like the play to make.

Robin Pollock-Daniel: A C D D N N S

CANDY (14A, 22, 186)

Plays like DAD and DAN (C3) are inferior because of the four-consonant leave. CANDY is a clear choice.

. . . .

5.   **John Luebkemann: E E I I R T W**

WIDE (D12, 31, 156)

Perfect, as it maximizes the score while producing an ideal leave from these tiles.

Robin Pollock-Daniel: D E H J N O S

JOSHED (J5, 36, 222)

It's either this play or HON (F10, 34). JOSHED dispenses with the S for an extra 2 points and adds possibility to the board. Indeed, John averages about 6 more points after Robin plays JOSHED than after she plays HON. On the other hand, Robin averages over 8 more points on her next turn after JOSHED than after HON. The two plays are about equal, but I think that I would opt for HON in this case, as it gives Robin a 64-point lead while retaining the S hook at J7.

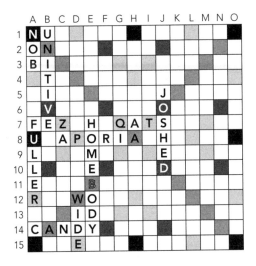

......

6. John Luebkemann: D E I M R S T

HERMIT (8J, 36, 192)

> *A nice-looking rack, though no bingo. HERMIT scores well but gives Robin much more to work with and also ruins a promising bingo rack. At the least, REMIT (F8, 34) is a better play. However, and especially given John's deficit, RIM (F8, 25) and BID (3A, 12) should be considered. The EIMRST leave after BID is fantastic, and according to Quackle, John bingos an incredible 86 percent of the time on his next move. Nevertheless, Robin would be likely to play more defensively than Quackle after John's obvious fishing play. Not an easy decision.*

Robin Pollock-Daniel: E I I K N U X

XI (F10, 51, 273)

> *This "obvious" play simulates almost 5 points worse than JUNKIE (5J, 34), and it is not hard to see why: the IX is retained for F10 XI next turn, and it is harder for John to play a bingo. Also, Robin's leave is very likely to be stronger after JUNKIE than after XI.*

7. John Luebkemann: B D L O R S ☐
   OILB<u>I</u>RDS (N7, 82, 274)
   > *A quality play.*

   Robin Pollock-Daniel: E F I K N U W
   FUNKIER (12H, 36, 309)
   > *Best. FUJI (5H, 28) is a possibility, but I would rather take out a few*
   > *bingo lines and not keep both a K and a W.*

....

8. John Luebkemann: A E E G G I R
   REJIG (5H, 26, 300)
   > *One of several decent plays: JIG (5J, 22), JAGG (5J, 22), JAGGER,*
   > *JIGGER, or JAEGER (5J, 30), and GAM (9C, 27). With three O's still*
   > *to come, it might be prudent to make a play using the J. However, GEM*
   > *(9C, 27) is probably best. The leave of AEGIR would go well with quite*
   > *a number of low-point tiles still unseen. In addition, GEM guarantees a*
   > *good score next turn, either using the J or playing vertically from the F*
   > *at H12 (FRAG at a minimum).*

   Robin Pollock-Daniel: A I P T T W Y
   PATTY (4K, 38, 347)

....

9. John Luebkemann: A C E G L N V
   Unseen tiles: A A A E E E G I N O O O R S S T U W
   CAVY (O1, 36, 336)
   > *It is either this play or CAVER (H1, 33). I like CAVY better; despite*
   > *the fact that there are eleven vowels and only seven consonants unseen,*
   > *it is better to keep an E with the GLN combo.*

   Robin Pollock-Daniel: E E E I O U W
   Unseen tiles: A A A E G G L N N O O R S S T
   UKE (K11, 14, 361)
   > *Ugh. After playing PATTY, Robin picks EEEOU from the bag. This*
   > *results in a very difficult situation for her.*
   > *Robin's play of UKE reduces John's chances of playing a bingo*
   > *drastically by taking out his most likely location (row 14). However,*

he is likely to forge ahead anyway because, from Robin's vantage point, he almost assuredly holds a nice mix of low-point tiles. Quackle recommends exchanging all tiles except EI, but I think that Robin's play is better here. Nevertheless, she will have to get lucky to win this game.

....

10. **John Luebkemann: A A E G L N S**
    Unseen tiles: A E E G I N O O O R S T W
    GAM (9M, 27, 363)

    Ideal: he maximizes his score and retains a beautiful rack. Incidentally, he would have had the bingo LASAGNES had Robin not blocked with UKE.

    Robin Pollock-Daniel: E E I N O O W
    Unseen tiles: A A E G L N O R S S T
    TWOONIE (4B, 25, 386)

    It's either this play or WOOER (H1, 27). Regardless, John likely has at least one S for a big play hooking REJIG. Perhaps Robin will be able to then play from the F at H12 to hold on to the win.

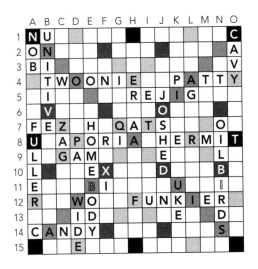

11.   John Luebkemann: A A E L N S S
      Unseen tiles: E G O R T
      FANE (H12, 21, 384)

> *John now threatens both SLATS (M1, 24) and LASS (3E, 15). If he had played SLATS first, Robin would have won the game with ERGOTS (1H, 24).*

   Robin Pollock-Daniel: E G O R T
   GROT (M1, 10, 396)

> *BIOG (3A, 27) loses by 1 point!*

. . . .

12.   John Luebkemann: A L S S
      LASS (3E, 15, 399)

> *+4 for the ET on Robin's rack: 403*

Final score: John Luebkemann 403, Robin Pollock-Daniel 396

Game #5: Seesaw

Joel Wapnick vs. Rod MacNeil
Can-Am Challenge, 2008

Another exciting game, decided only near the end.

....

1.   **Joel Wapnick: A E E O U X Z**
     ZOEAE (8D, 48, 48)
     Rod MacNeil: C E O O O R V
     Exchange OOOV (0, 0)

> *Way too pessimistic. ZOO (D8, 12) produces a leave of COVER, which
> has a solid valuation of +6.69. ZOO simulates over ten points better
> than the exchange.*

....

2.   **Joel Wapnick: A D I L N U X**
     LAX (9C, 31, 79)

> *Not anywhere near as good as ADIEUX (F5, 34), which cleans out the
> rack and maximizes the score at the same time.*

     Rod MacNeil: B C E R S W Y
     CRY (7E, 35, 35)

....

3.   **Joel Wapnick: D D I N O T U**
     DURE (F5, 7, 86)

> *Incredible: the highest-scoring play nets only 10 points! UDO (10A,
> 10), DUD, DUO, DUIT, DUI, DONUT (all at 9H) and my play all
> simulate within 2 points of each other. I chose DURE because with a
> lead, I wanted to keep the board closed as much as I could.*

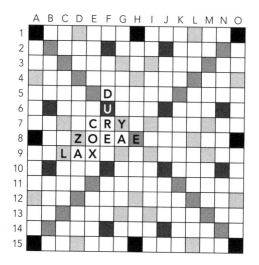

Rod MacNeil: B E I S W W Y

YWIS (10A, 32, 67)

> *An interesting situation: play the Y or hold it back for the hook on the next play? Both IWIS and YWIS are OSPD-acceptable words, and Rod probably played YWIS because he figured that it was likely that I would have an I on my rack, which I did. However, placing the Y in column A is just as damaging and no longer requires an I to make a play covering one of the two triple word scores.*

....

4. Joel Wapnick: D I L N O T T

DOTTILY (A4, 39, 125)

Rod MacNeil: A B E E I V W

VIEW (B2, 28, 95)

> *His best play. WAIVE (E1, 28) has a better leave, but placing the W in a triple word row, on an otherwise fairly closed board, has its drawbacks.*

....

5. **Joel Wapnick: A I J L N O P**

JO (E4, 24, 149)

> *Better than JIAO (E2, 28), which leaves three consonants. ADJOIN*
> *(5E, 28) is of course way too dangerous. It takes a T as well as an S.*

Rod MacNeil: A A E E B M S

BEAM (C4, 23, 118)

> *Another best play. It remains to be seen whether this game will break*
> *out into a barn burner or will stay cramped and gnarled all the way to*
> *the end.*

....

6. **Joel Wapnick: A A F I L N P**

PLAIN (9G, 24, 173)

> *I never like being the first one to open a closed board, but had I*
> *not done so, there was a chance anyway that Rod might have had a*
> *bingo from 9G or 9H. PLAIN scores better than anything else, and*
> *provisionally gives me a nice place for my F (10J).*

Rod MacNeil: A D E M O R S

MADRONES (K4, 94, 212)

> *Damn! I should have played FA (G4, 9). Actually, he would have had*
> *RADOMES (9H) had I done that.*

....

7. **Joel Wapnick: A A F Q T T V**

QAT (L3, 34, 207)

> *Quackle favors FAVA (L1, 36) over QAT by 3 points, with FETA (10J,*
> *28) another point back of QAT. I respectfully disagree. True, Rod may have*
> *a big play coming back if he has an I for QI, and true, there are three U's*
> *unseen. Nevertheless, QTT is an ugly, ugly leave. AFTV is not much better,*
> *but at least I didn't have to worry about getting rid of the albatross Q.*

Rod MacNeil: E H I N O O U

HIE (M2, 39, 251)

> *Rod's play scores a bunch of points and is best. Nevertheless, that*
> *NOUU rack is not a thing of beauty. I would have made the same play,*
> *though HEINOUS (11E, 20) is worthy of some consideration.*

8. **Joel Wapnick: A A F G T T V**

FETA (10J, 28, 235)

> *Or FET or FEAT in the same spot. FETA outperforms FEAT by a scant point in the simulation, with FET another point and a half back. Keeping the doubled A's is not good, but fortunately only one A remains unseen.*

Rod MacNeil: K N O O U U ☐

KURU (7I, 13, 264)

> *An interesting choice between KURU and KORUN (7I, 15). KORUN appears to be the more defensive play, given that it takes only an A, not an S. But according to Quackle, the probability of Rod playing a bingo the following turn is only 1.5 percent lower if he plays KORUN versus if he plays KURU. Quackle has KORUN ahead in the simulation, but I don't believe it. KURU is the play.*

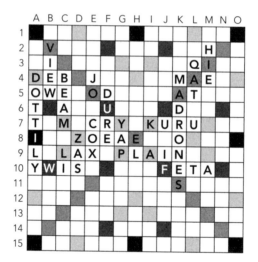

9. **Joel Wapnick: A E E G R T V**

VAU (J5, 19, 254)

Another interesting situation: among the thirty-six unseen tiles are two S's and two blanks. My VAU was an attempt to retain a decent rack and not open anything for Rod. Better would have been GAVE (M9, 10). It retains an ideal leave and makes it somewhat difficult for Rod to bingo.

Rod MacNeil: E L N N O O ☐

ON (B7, 9, 273)

Very well thought out. Instead of opening the board with a play like WOOLEN (B10, 18), he keeps it closed while retaining a balanced rack that includes the last L, for a hook at N10.

---

10. **Joel Wapnick: E E G I N R T**

EVERTING (2A, 64, 318)

With two blanks and two S's unseen, from my perspective, GRATINEE (M8, 70) is out of the question.

Rod MacNeil: D E L N O O ☐

C̲ONDOLE (N5, 71, 344)

The best bingo, as the C restricts possible counterplay down column O more than the other possibilities (e.g., E̲I̲DOLON, ONE̲F̲OLD, NOODLE̲S̲, NOODLE̲D̲, and S̲NOOLED).

---

11. **Joel Wapnick: A E H N P S U**

Unseen tiles: B C E E F G G I I I N O R R R S T

HAEN (O6, 39, 357)

HEAP (1F, 43) is better. There is no good reason not to take the extra points right now.

Quackle likes WHAUP (B10, 26). If I had been farther behind than I was, this would have been a great play. However, I felt that I had a good chance to win without opening up the board and playing for a bingo. Given that there was a 39 percent chance of Rod drawing the blank after he played C̲ONDOLE, why take chances?

Rod MacNeil: C G I N R R □

Unseen tiles: B E E F G I I O P R S S T U

GIRN (12N, 20, 364)

> *Perhaps Rod made this play in order to kill O11–O15 for me (e.g., SPIRT, FUGIO, etc.). Regardless, it was a mistake. There are other places on this board for me to score well. CARING (M9, 34) was the play.*
>
> *Quackle rates WRING (B10, 18) as high as CARING, but with two S's unseen for a hook into the triple word score row at the bottom of the board, I see no reason to take such a risk.*

....

12. Joel Wapnick: B E I P S S U

Unseen tiles: C E F G I O R R T □

BIS (N1, 32, 389)

> *On this closed-down board, I was intent on emptying the bag so that Rod could not set himself up. Yes, sometimes it is better not to leave a tile in the bag. PIS is just as good as BIS.*

Rod MacNeil: C F I R R T □

My rack: E E G O P S U

ARC (1H, 18, 382)

> *I am threatening to play OP (O1, 32). Given that AFRIT (1H, 30), MAFIC (M9, 25), and Rod's play lead nowhere—that is, he will not be able to play out next turn on any of these plays, nor will he score well—why not block my OP with IT? I would still have a winning sequence, but it would be hard to see over the board with limited time.*
>
> *My winning sequence, had Rod played IT, consists of playing GUESS (11G) followed by NOPE (O12), or of playing UPO (1E, 13) followed by LIEGES (C9).*

....

13. Joel Wapnick: E E G O P S U

OP (O1, 32, 421)

> *No fancy out-in-two for me.*

Rod MacNeil: F I R T

FON (9M, 19, 401)

....

14. Joel Wapnick: E E G S U
    US (10F, 13, 434)
    Rod MacNeil: I R T
    WRIT (B10, 7, 408)
        +8 for the EEG on Joel's rack: 416
        −10 for going overtime: 406

Final score: Joel Wapnick 434, Rod MacNeil 406

Game #6: Squeaker #2

Noah Walton vs. Dave Wiegand
Reno Summer Tournament, 2009

A barn burner of a game between the man who would win the 2009 National
SCRABBLE Championship a month after this game was played (Wiegand)
and an up-and-coming expert who was still in high school.

....

1. **Noah Walton: B E I J N R U**
    JIBER (8D, 44, 44)
    Dave Wiegand: A D N O R T □
    RATION<u>E</u>D (E5, 82, 82)

    > *AROINTED is a little safer than the other double-double bingos
    > (RATIONED, ORDINATE, ANTIDORA), as it avoids placing a
    > vowel next to either of the triple letter scores at F6 and F10.*

....

2. **Noah Walton: B E N O P T U**
    BOP (D11, 23, 67)

    > *Bottleneck at the top: Noah's play, BOUND (12A, 22), BOB (F6, 25),
    > and UPON (D10, 23) all simulate within three-tenths of a point of
    > each other. My personal preference is BOUND, because it sheds both the
    > B and the U.*

    Dave Wiegand: D F L M N Q U
    FLAM (6C, 15, 97)

    > *I think that QUALM is a better play here. Yes, there is a small danger
    > that Noah might hook it with a Y or an S, but it is worth it to get rid of
    > the Q, even though Dave has a U on his rack to go along with it.*

....

3. **Noah Walton: A E I N T U W**

WAIF (C3, 20, 87)

> *Quackle prefers WAE to WAIF by less than a point, but I think that WAIF is correct nevertheless. Holding on to the E is more important that taking the two extra points.*

Dave Wiegand: D N O Q U W X

QUOD (D1, 59, 156)

> *So much for my advice recommending QUALM over FLAM!*

4. **Noah Walton: E I N T T U V**

QUINT (1D, 42, 129)

> *ETV is a better leave than the V by itself, but only by about 3 points. Thus QUINTET should be the better play as it outscores QUINT by 6 points. And in fact, QUINTET simulates 3 points better than QUINT.*

Dave Wiegand: A N N R W X Y

WAXY (7G, 40, 196)

> *The cost for undoubling the N's is a minimum of 11 points. That is too much, and so Dave's play is correct. WAX (7G, 36) holds back the Y hook for next turn. It is a nice idea and might be worth it if the J column had a nearby double word score square. Quackle rates WAXY about 3 points higher than WAX.*

5. **Noah Walton: C E E I N T V**

EVICT (I1, 26, 155)

> *EVINCE (8J, 41) scores way more points than anything else and is even a better play now, with Noah behind, than if the game scores were closer to each other.*

Dave Wiegand: I N N R R S T

WORN (3C, 7, 203)

> *Only 7 points, but a terrific play. The INRST leave has great potential.*

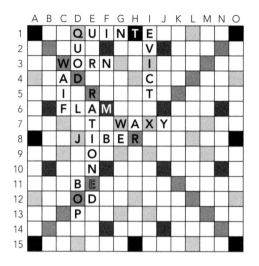

---

6. **Noah Walton: A A E E N O U**

Exchange AEOU (0, 155)

> *A little too pessimistic: EAU (F11, 11) or even AFLAME (6B, 19) are worth playing. But if he must exchange, then I like keeping EN rather than AEN. There are still plenty of vowels remaining in the bag, and the ratio of unseen consonant to vowels—30 to 22—is not high enough to justify keeping the two vowels with the one consonant.*

Dave Wiegand: A I N R S T Y

BY (F8, 12, 215)

> *According to Quackle, there is an 84 percent probability that Dave will play a bingo on the turn following this one if he plays BY. After BRAY (F8, 24), it is a 58 percent probability. On the other hand, Dave's last two plays indicate that he is close to a bingo. Noah should play defensively unless . . .*

....

7.   **Noah Walton: A C D E I N O**
CATENOID (5G, 72, 227)

>   *. . . he has a bingo!*

Dave Wiegand: A E I N R S T
NASTIER (O3, 86, 301)

....

8.   **Noah Walton: A E E L O S T**
OLEATES (N9, 70, 297)

>   *Boom. The board looks a lot different now than it did three turns ago.*

Dave Wiegand: E G H H I L S
SLEIGHS (15H, 39, 340)

>   *Good play. Even though he sacrifices the S for 5 points versus HEIGHT*
>   *(13I, 34), he takes away a dangerous spot from Noah's consideration.*

....

9.   **Noah Walton: K N P R R T V**
PRINK (M3, 32, 329)

>   *A good example of how one free vowel can fix a rack full of consonants.*

Dave Wiegand: D E G H O S U
DOUGHT (13I, 26, 366)

>   *He holds SOUGHED with no place to play it. DOUGHT is a fine*
>   *play, as it cuts off bingo lines and retains a good leave.*

....

10. **Noah Walton: A E I L R T V**
Unseen tiles: A A E E E E F G I M O O S U Z
LEVIRATE (11G, 72, 401)

>   *Not RELATIVE, as that play might create a very lucrative comeback*
>   *for Dave if he has the Z and an A—which, as it turns out, he does.*

	A	B	C	D	E	F	G	H	I	J	K	L	M	N	O
1				Q	U	I	N	T	E						
2				U				V							
3			W	O	R	N			I				P		N
4			A	D				C					R		A
5			I		R		C	A	T	E	N	O	I	D	S
6			F	L	A	M							N		T
7				T			W	A	X	Y			K		I
8				J	I	B	E	R							E
9				O	Y								O		R
10				N									L		
11			B	E		L	E	V	I	R	A	T	E		
12			O	D									A		
13			P					D	O	U	G	H	T		
14													E		
15								S	L	E	I	G	H	S	

Dave Wiegand: A A E E O S Z

Unseen tiles: E E F G I M O U ☐

ZOEA (14F, 39, 405)

> *Down by 35 points with five vowels on his rack and a seven-of-nine chance that Noah has the blank, Dave is in trouble. He has only two viable choices: ZOEA and ZOEAS (14F, 47). I'd play ZOEAS and hope for two consonants to play out with, or for a consonant and the blank.*

---

11. **Noah Walton: E G I M O U ☐**

Wiegand's rack: A E E F S

MOGUL (C10, 31, 432)

> *Good play, though GOMUTI (C10, 34) is even better. It wins by 11 if Dave follows with FEASE (9H), and 13 if Dave plays SEIF (15A) and Noah then plays BYE (F8).*

Dave Wiegand: A E E F S

AVE (2H, 10, 415)

> *Dave has a spot to play out—FEASE (9H, 15)—but he will lose by more than he actually does lose by if he takes it. He blocks Noah's out play of VIE by playing AVE.*

12.　　Noah Walton: E I
　　　　BYE (F8, 14, 446)
　　　　　　Just enough to win.
　　　　Dave Wiegand: E F S
　　　　FES (15A, 26, 441)
　　　　　　+2 for the I on Noah's rack: 443

Final score: Noah Walton 446, Dave Wiegand 443

Game #7: Squeaker #3

Jason Katz-Brown vs. Lloyd Mills
Can-Am Challenge, 2006

A game that illustrates why it is not always correct to play the bingo.

....

1. **Jason Katz-Brown: A E G I I L T**
    AGILE (8D, 14, 14)

    > *The best play here is a nonplay: exchange the I. AIGLET isn't the
    > world's best six-letter stem, though it forms bingos with D, E, K, L, N,
    > and S, or about 30 percent of the tile pool. However, Jason's plays are
    > all low scoring, and their leaves are nothing to write home about either.
    > Also, if Lloyd plays almost anything in response to a one-tile fish, it is
    > likely to increase Jason's chances of playing a bingo next turn.*
    >
    > > *AGILE is Jason's best non-exchange play, almost 6 points worse
    > than exchanging the I.*

    Lloyd Mills: K L N O R R U
    KORUNA (D3, 20, 20)

....

2. **Jason Katz-Brown: E E H I J T ☐**
    JEU (6B, 26, 40)
    Lloyd Mills: E L P R V V Z
    VERVE (H4, 15, 35)

    > *Tough choice. PREZ (5C, 34) scores well but results in a leave that
    > is about 18 points worse than the LPZ leave after Lloyd's VERVE.
    > However, PREZ outscores VERVE by 19. Even though PREZ comes out
    > best in the Quackle simulation, keeping the two V's is awful, and there
    > is a very good chance that Lloyd would have had to exchange tiles the
    > following turn. I would go with Lloyd's play.*

3.   **Jason Katz-Brown: E H I I I T ☐**

TIKE (3B, 16, 56)

I wonder if Jason picked the wrong tile off his rack by accident. TIKI in the same spot is obviously better. It is also the best play.

Lloyd Mills: A I L P T W Z

ZIP (2A, 36)

ZAP is a couple of points worse. Duplicate I's are worse than duplicate A's.

---

4.   **Jason Katz-Brown: G G H I I L ☐**

GIGGLI$\underline{S}$H (E8: challenged off)

GIGGLISH is not one of the great plausible phonies. He should have played VIGIL (4H, 18) right away.

Lloyd Mills: A A D L T U W

WARD (6F, 16, 87)

The U and W are the oil and water of SCRABBLE. They just don't mix at all. When together on the same rack, it is imperative to get rid of one of them immediately.

WARD is a decent play, but it is hard to see why DRAW (5C, 19), with its extra 3 points, or TWA (9H, 22), with its extra 6 points, should not be played instead. And besides, why give Jason a bingo opportunity?

....

5. **Jason Katz-Brown:** G G H I I L ☐

VIGIL (4H, 18, 74)

Wow, what a word Jason missed—WHIRLIGIG (F6, 72)!

Lloyd Mills: A D I L O T U

OUTLAID (2E, 64, 151)

The only bingo.

....

6. **Jason Katz-Brown:** A E E G H N ☐

THENAGE (1L, 92, 166)

Outstanding play.

Lloyd Mills: A E O B C S ☐

ICEBOATS (K4, 94, 245)

Another outstanding one.

....

7. **Jason Katz-Brown:** A F O R S S W

SOWARS (8J, 39, 205)

His move is good, but even better is the stunning SOFAS (9D, 43). Its
RW leave is about 3 points better than the FO leave after Jason's play.

Lloyd Mills: A A E I O Q U

QUAIS (O4, 24, 269)

> *Given that the three-vowel leaves of EIO and AEO are comparable,*
> *Lloyd might as well take the extra 4 points for AQUA (3L, 28). As for*
> *ROQUE (N8, 34), not only is its leave of AAI inferior—it has all kinds*
> *of defensive weaknesses.*

---

8.   **Jason Katz-Brown: F H M N N O Y**

HORNY (N6, 42, 247)

> *Easily best.*

Lloyd Mills: A E O O T T U

OUTATE (O10, 26, 295)

---

9.   **Jason Katz-Brown: F M N N O R S**

INFORM (F8, 19, 266)

> *Fine play, especially as he holds the last remaining S. Jason is behind,*
> *and thus has to keep the board open and hope for the best.*

Lloyd Mills: B D L M O R Y

Unseen tiles: A C D E E E E F I I N N O P R S T T X

YOM (E11, 34, 329)

> *A good high-scoring blocking play, appropriate for someone striving to*
> *maintain a lead. The four-consonant leave is worrisome, however.*

---

10.   **Jason Katz-Brown: E E F N O P S**

Unseen tiles: A B C D D E E I I L N R R T T X

POMME (13C, 24, 290)

> *Jason springs a phony, possibly confusing the French word for apple with*
> *POMMEE, which is acceptable. This phony is more convincing than*
> *GIGGLISH, and Lloyd lets it go. Better would have been FEMME*
> *(13C, 26). Quackle is partial to FEN (N13, 23), presumably for its nice*
> *leave. However, it leaves Jason nowhere to bingo except off the J. But*
> *FEMME creates a hook location at 14G for a possible bingo. FEN is the*
> *play when ahead, and FEMME is best when behind.*

Lloyd Mills: B D D L R R T

Unseen tiles: A C E E E F I I N N S T X

DORR (12D, 18, 347)

> There are six tiles in the bag, so Lloyd cannot exchange tiles even if he
> wanted to. His DORR is a fine play—he scores decently and doesn't get
> suckered into playing into row 15 (e.g., DOLT, D12).

....

11. **Jason Katz-Brown: C E F N N S T**

Unseen tiles: A B D E E I I L R T X

VERVET (H4, 12, 302)

> He rightly eschews the 40-point play SECT (H12). It would put him
> within 17 points, but with a leave of FNN plus three unknown tiles,
> it is very hard to see how he could win. With VERVET, he gambles on
> picking one of the two remaining E's for FENNECS.

Lloyd Mills: B D E I L R T

Unseen tiles: A C E E F I N N S X

DRIBLET (14G, 70, 417)

> Believe it or not, the bingo is a mistake. According to Quackle, Jason
> will play a bingo 16 percent of the time after DRIBLET. However,

Jason has just played away one tile. He is bingo fishing, and his chance of playing one on his next turn is thus way higher than Quackle's figure, which is based on a random draw of seven of the ten unseen tiles. The real problem for Lloyd is that some of these bingos are very high scoring—high enough to win. For example, ANNEXES (15A, 100) wins by 1 point, and FIANCEE (15B, 100) and FASCINE or FANCIES (15A, 100) win by five. INCENSE (15B, 97) wins by eight.

Lloyd's best play here is LIB (H13, 27), which allows no bingos. Of course one would have to be a genius to be able to figure that out over the board. Incidentally, a play like BID (N13, 23) could potentially lose to a bingo starting at I9 (ANNEXES and INCENSE). It is much less risky than DRIBLET, but riskier than LIB.

....

12.   Jason Katz-Brown: C E E F N N S
FENNECS (15A, 94, 396)
+20 for the AIX on Lloyd's rack: 416

Final score: Lloyd Mills 417, Jason Katz-Brown 416

What a game!

Game #8: Ironic Endgame

Joey Mallick vs. Adam Logan
Can-Am Challenge, 2006

This was a low-scoring game, but it was chock full of interesting choices.

....

1. **Joey Mallick:** N O O R S T Y

   OY (8H, 10, 10)

   > *NORST is a fine leave, but the NS leave is 7 points worse and scores an extra 14. I would go with ROOTY.*

   Adam Logan: A D I T V W W

   WAW (7H, 21, 21)

   > *Above or below? The 9H location actually simulates a point higher than Adam's 7H play (after 10,000 iterations). Perhaps it is slightly easier for Joey to make a parallel play along row 9 after the 7H play than it would be for him to make a parallel play along row 7 after the 9H play.*

....

2. **Joey Mallick:** M N N O R S T

   MORN (6I, 23, 33)

   Adam Logan: D I R R R T V

   Exchange DIRRV (0, 21)

   > *WORRIT (H7, 10) is worthy of consideration. Nevertheless, it scores only 10 points, does not get rid of the V, and gives Joey a couple of tiles to play through. VROW (J4, 10) is another possibility, but the DIRRT leave is uninspiring. I like Adam's choice. Keeping IRT and DIRT appear to be equally good as Adam's decision to keep RT.*

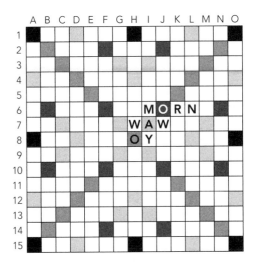

....

3. **Joey Mallick: C I N R S S T**

RINS (9F, 22, 55)

> *Right place, wrong move. Given that Joey holds another S, he might as*
> *well make a play that can be hooked with it. NITS (9F, 22) is the play.*
> *RINS simulates a full 4 points worse.*

Adam Logan: A G O O R R T

ARGOT (E7, 18, 39)

> *It is interesting to note than AGOROT (E8, 20) simulates higher than*
> *ARGOT. One might think that OR is a nicer leave than R alone, but it*
> *turns out not to be the case: R is worth an extra 1½ points.*
>
> *An alternative to AGOROT is ROOT (5J, 20), which retains the*
> *G for E9. Six of one, half dozen of the other. I would play AGOROT for*
> *the extra two chances at drawing a blank or an S.*

....

4.   **Joey Mallick: I I I C S T T**

INTI (L5, 5, 60)

> *Missing the T hook at 10I. TITI (10I, 16) is the play.*

Adam Logan: H I I O O R V

Exchange HIIOOV (0, 39)

> *Way too pessimistic in view of RHO (F9, 29).*

....

5.   **Joey Mallick: B C E I N S T**

BOY (8G, 12, 72)

> *Good play—CEINST is a dynamite rack, worth about 35 points. Joey's fishing play is way better than anything else, including the 24-point plays from 8A to 8E.*

Adam Logan: D E R R T U ☐

TORTURED (11E, 66, 105)

> *Quackle recommends TRUDGER (M8, 68), and this play actually comes out on top in the simulation by 1½ points over Adam's play. I would never leave the S hook into a triple word score for just an extra 2 points, and I would especially not do so after a play like Joey's one-tile fishing expedition. Adam's play is best.*

....

6.   **Joey Mallick: C E I N S T U**

TUNIC (H11, 24, 96)

> *A disappointment, to say the least—Joey had NEUSTIC at 12B and across the board at M8, but Adam's bingo blocked both spots. Of the four plays that are virtually tied in the simulation, I prefer Joey's play or INCUR (8A, 24) to CUTER (8A, 24) because of the superior EST leave compared to INS. However, I really like CRU (J10, 11). The EINST leave is great, and after CRU there are two good locations for bingos.*

Adam Logan: A A I O U V X

ROUX (J11, 27, 132)

> *IXIA (8L, 33) is another possibility, but the UV combination in the leave is death. Despite outscoring ROUX by 6 points, ROUX simulates 2 points higher.*

···

7. **Joey Mallick: A E F M S S T**
FAMES (12A, 35, 131)
Adam Logan: A A I K L O V
KALIF (A8, 36, 168)

> *This would have been a great play if Adam had retained two of ATE for a shot at KALIFATE. Of the two best moves, KOALA (B10, 38) and ALFAKI (A10, 39), KOALA seems a tad better because of its superior defensive nature.*

···

8. **Joey Mallick: L O S S T T Y**
STY (13A, 41, 172)

> *Fine play, as it scores well while retaining the lone vowel.*

Adam Logan: A D E N O O V
NOVAE (D4, 23, 191)

> *VIDEO (8K, 27) is slightly superior to other plays, such as Adam's NOVAE, VOID (5J, 29), and the pretty DONATE (B9, 27). The valuation of its leave is only 1½ points worse than the valuation of NOVAE's leave.*

···

9. **Joey Mallick: L N O P R S T**
LOIN (5J, 18, 190)

> *Another decent play. Nevertheless, PILOT (8K, 21) scores a few extra points and has the advantage of retaining a three-consonant leave rather than a four-consonant one. POINT (5J, 26) should be avoided because POINTE is a word and there are nine E's yet unplayed.*

Adam Logan: A D F G L O V
FLAG (B6, 25, 216)

> *There are no decent plays that get rid of the V, which is unfortunate for Adam. FLAG seems best. LOAF (E2, 26) results in an awkward DGV leave, and while moves like FLOG (4G) and FOG (4H) set up the A nicely (AGLOW, J3), it must be remembered that there are three A's unseen. Joey may well use the spot before Adam gets a chance at it.*

10. Joey Mallick: A E P R S T T
    PATTERS (F1, 66, 256)

> *TAPSTER (N2, 77) scores an additional 11 points, SPATTER (N5, 72) an additional 6. Moreover, Joey's play of PATTERS places the P right in the middle of a triple word score row. It simulates 14 points worse than TAPSTER, and deservedly so.*

   Adam Logan: C D E N O V ☐
   VOIDANCE (2B, 76, 292)

> *The only other bingo, CONCAVED or CONCAVED (2B, 76), is way more dangerous because of the exposed E at 2H, right below the triple word score.*

> *Two A's remain unseen. Will one of the players hook one of them at 2A?*

11. Joey Mallick: A E E E E H L
    ECHE (H1, 30, 286)

> *Excellent play. The odds are against Adam having the last A, so maybe Joey can play there next turn. Besides, who wants an EEE leave, especially with three more E's unseen?*

   Adam Logan: D G H J I I U
   Unseen tiles: A A B D E E E E E I I L O P Q Z
   DJIN (M2, 24, 316)

> *HIP (1D, 23) is the play. Its leave, though nothing to write home about, is about 3 points better than DJIN.*

12. Joey Mallick: A A E E E E L
    Unseen tiles: B D E G H I I I O P Q U Z
    AJEE (3L, 11, 297)

> *This play informs Adam that Joey holds the other A. Otherwise, Joey certainly would have saved the one he played by playing JEE (3M) instead. AJEE brings Joey within 19, seems extremely dangerous, yet simulates highest. Why? First, it is the only reasonable play that retains a consonant in the leave! With six vowels and seven consonants unseen, it is*

important to hold on to the consonant. And second, it gives him a chance
to draw one of the heavy tiles, preferably the Z, for a killer play down
from A1.

Adam Logan: D G H I I Q U
Unseen tiles: A B E E E I L O P Z
HIED (O1, 30, 346)

Nursing a small lead, Adam feels that he must take out column O.
Quackle strongly recommends HI (K13, 19), for the simple reason that
if Adam draws one of the three unseen E's, he will have the 81-point
EQUID (15K) next turn. But how many points do you need to win by?
HIED puts Adam up by 49, and unless Joey comes up with a gigantic Z
play (e.g., BAIZE, A1, too many points to count), Adam should be able
to hold on.

Incidentally, this game has a humorous aspect to it. Each player
needs what the other has, and as it turns out, neither will get what he
needs! Adam would love to have an A for QAID (A1), and Joey would
very much want any of the high-point tiles still in play except the Q. As
we will see, all of them will go to Adam.

13. Joey Mallick: A E E E I O L

EDILE (L10, 12, 309)

> *Great play, as Joey will be able to play out next turn, catching Adam with either the Q or the Z. Holding AEO, he will have two out plays.*

Adam Logan: B G I P Q U Z

ZIP (8K, 14, 360)

> *QUIN (4A, 23) gives Adam a bit more breathing room.*

....

14. Joey Mallick: A E O

TOEA (7L, 10, 319)

> *The other out play was AEON (4A, 5).*
> *+34 for the BGIQU on Adam's rack: 353*

Final score: Adam Logan 360, Joey Mallick 353

CHAPTER 9

Cool Plays

This quiz presents positions in which clever plays were found either over the board or from postgame analysis. These include unusual bingos, unexpected inside plays, multiple overlaps, strategic gems, setup plays, and endgame maneuvers.

These plays range from fine moves that are somewhat difficult to find, to dazzling and unexpected brilliancies of considerably greater depth. See how many of them you can solve. Don't feel too smug if you discover most or all of them. Remember that you, unlike the original solvers of these problems, know that there is something to be found. It's much easier to find the needle if you know the haystack contains one.

Example #1

You: 313 | Opponent: 321

Your rack: A I K O R W Y

Solution: WORK (A1, 77). We begin with an easy one. Of course you will need to know that EVOCABLE takes an R front hook.

Example #2

You: 12 | Opponent: 109

Your rack: C E I J P R T

Solution: PIER (J7, 18). Spotted by Kenji Matsumoto. PIER sets up INJECT (8J, 69) for his next play.

Example #3

You: 405 | Opponent: 449

Your rack: A E E M N N R

Unseen tiles: G G I L N O O Z

Solution: INK (L4, 7). A terrific desperation play made Tim Adamson in a Can-Am Challenge Example against Evan Berofsky. Tim loses unless he plays a bingo. By dumping one of the two N's, he gave himself a 25 percent chance of winning. He picked one of the two O's, which enabled him to play either DEMEANOR (15D) or FORENAME (O8). Evan played DOZING (15D, 51) on his following turn, and Tim played FORENAME, winning 510 to 500.

How to Play SCRABBLE Like a Champion

Example #4

You: 146 | Opponent: 124

Your rack: E E I M N T T

Solution: THUNK (K9, 14). The first of three great setups from the same game. There are many decent plays that hook an I onto CAROL (e.g., MITTEN, 12D, 26), but THUNK is the best play by far. Its EEIMNT leave combines with seven different letters to form nine seven-letter bingos, including A, E, and O. Moreover, the bingos it forms with the vowels all end in E, for a vertical play at L4: ETAMINE, MATINEE, EREMITE, and ONETIME. Other bingos might also be playable through the I hook at 12E or through the other open tiles on the board.

Example #5

You: 203 | Opponent: 230

Your rack: E H P R S T V

Solution: VEX (G7, 17). EHPRST doesn't look like a great bingo-making machine. Nevertheless, it combines with lots of letters to make seven- and eight-letter bingos (e.g., TEPHRAS, THREEPS, POTHERS).

Example #6

You: 257 | Opponent: 254

Your rack: D E E F L S T

Solution: EF (4C, 20). Even though dumping the F indicates to the opponent that the player is fishing, a bingo next turn may be unstoppable. There are too many opportunities on this board for them.

DEELST forms bingos with A (DELATES), E (DELETES, SLEETED, STEELED), I (ISLETED), U (TELEDUS), and five consonants (SMELTED, NESTLED, PESTLED, SETTLED, and LEWDEST). In addition, there are many bingo possibilities through the F at 1H and the E and R of AVER.

Example #7

You: 20 | Opponent: 20

Your rack: A H I L N P R

Solution: ALPHORN (E5, 48). A double-double that extends HO in both directions.

How to Play SCRABBLE Like a Champion

Example #8

You: 336 | Opponent: 342

Your rack: D E E I L R U

Opponent's rack: E I L M N U ☐

I reached this position in a club game a few years ago. I needed to find a play that would meet three requirements: it would score decently, block my opponent's bingo of R̲ELUMINE or D̲EMILUNE (15H), and allow me to win the game by playing out on my next turn. BYLINED (I8, 22) fit the bill. Opponent's best play following BYLINED is one of the 30-point plays starting at 2J (MUS̲CLES, MINCE̲D, etc.), after which RUER (3C, 13) wins by three. Or if opponent plays ORMOLU (3E, 27) to block RUER, ECRU (2L, 12) wins by five.

Example #9

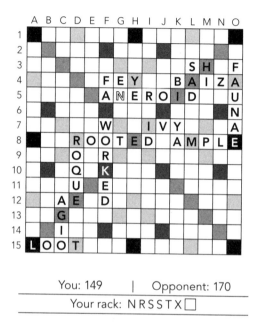

You: 149 | Opponent: 170

Your rack: N R S S T X ☐

Solution: YESTERN (H4, 20), from one of my long-ago tournament games. This play rids the rack of four of its six consonants by playing through YE and E while hooking a T onto IVY. I was rewarded by being able to play EXSERTS (B6) on my following play.

Example #10

	A	B	C	D	E	F	G	H	I	J	K	L	M	N	O
1															
2								D	U	D			S		
3								I					E		
4								T			W		J		
5								T		E	R		E		
6							D	O		X	I		A		
7							Y				N		N		
8							I	N	S	I	G	H	T		
9							N								
10							G								
11															
12															
13															
14															
15															

You: 97 | Opponent: 115

Your rack: E F I L N O P

Solution: PINOLE (N1, 41). A nice five-way overlap. A good play is OLEFIN (H10, 33), but PINOLE scores an extra 8 points and is perhaps safer.

Example #11

You: 298 | Opponent: 275

Your rack: E F I L M T Y

Solution: LIMY (14D, 39). There are a number of high-scoring plays here, but this one stands out from the crowd because of the nice way it sets up the F, and perhaps -FT, at 15D. The other interesting play is FLYTE (M3, 40)—pick one of the three unseen R's and MIRZA (8A, 48) could be the play next turn. Nevertheless, LIMY is best.

Example #12

You: 346 | Opponent: 392

Your rack: A E F N S S U

Opponent's rack: C L L O T

Solution: US (N2, 19). This position appeared in *Letters for Expert Game Players* almost thirty years ago, and was submitted by Joe Edley and Nick Ballard. I am grateful that changes in editions of the OSPD over the years have not cooked this situation!

Ballard wrote the following concerning the consequences of playing US: "If opponent plays OTIC (B6) for 8 = 400, threatening to go out with BILL (H10), you go out with FANES (12A) [to tie]. . . . You also tie with the same play if opponent plays COL (5G) for 8, threatening to go out with TIL (B7)." Ballard also noted that BLIN (I8) loses by 2 to FANES, VOLT (A8) fails against FANE (1L, 36), and COIL (B6, 12) leads to a 418–418 tie after FANE (1L), opponent's BLIN (I8) and your SQUAD (14I). All options other than US, including INFUSES (B8, 36); FANES, FAUNS, or FUSES (12A, 31); FUSE, FUSS, or FESS (N1, 29); INFUSE (I10, 25); and STAR (12L, 24) lose to opponent's best play. To summarize, US at least ties, which is remarkable considering the 46-point deficit before playing it.

Is it realistic to expect an expert player to find a play such as US over the board? In response to this problem, Steve Williams wrote: "The luxury of analyzing each play by yourself and your opponent is not available to the player who must produce points against time and pressure."

(continued on next page)

Example #13

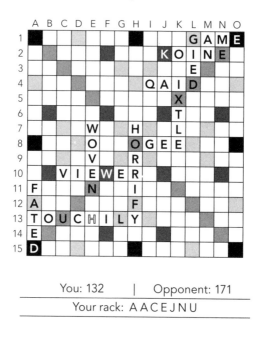

You: 132 | Opponent: 171

Your rack: A A C E J N U

(continued from previous page)

"The real issue is that the player give a worthy account of himself and his game by making it close. Win, lose, or draw, he can hold his head high—the game, thank heaven, is still played by human beings."

I agree with these sentiments, but nonetheless I believe that a strong expert should be able to find plays like US—not by calculating out all of the variations, but by thinking in terms of strategic principles. US does two things that no other play accomplishes: it creates a high-scoring setup that the opponent can neither use nor block (FANE, 1L), and it allows the option of playing out with FANES (12A), if necessary. In a timed game situation one might be unsure of the ultimate outcome after playing US, but careful consideration from a strategic viewpoint should make one certain that US is the best chance for winning. Very instructive!

Solution (this page): ACAJOU (8A, 69). From a game I played against the great Robert Felt in one of the Grand Canyon tournaments.

Example #14

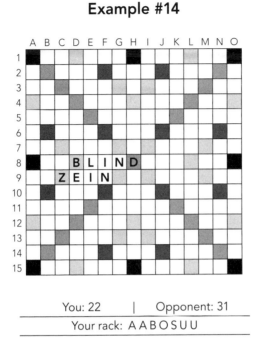

You: 22 | Opponent: 31

Your rack: A A B O S U U

Solution: ABOULIAS (E4, 40). This move, which was played by Robert Felt in a club game, is thematically similar to my play of ALPHORN a few positions back.

Example #15

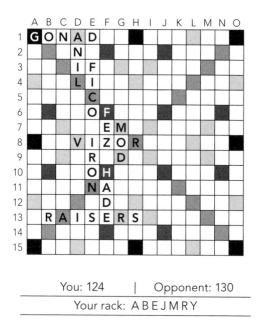

You: 124 | Opponent: 130

Your rack: A B E J M R Y

Solution: JAMBED (12A, 72). JERRY (B10, 62) is a nice scoring play, but JAMBED is even better—and prettier.

Example #16

You: 298 | Opponent: 274

Your rack: A E F G I Q R

Opponent's last play: ETA (9I, 3)

Unseen tiles: A C C E E I I L N N S T U

Solution: NEG (3I, 4). This move was made by Bradley Whitmarsh in a game from the winter 2009 Saratoga Springs tournament. His opponent was Paul Avrin. In Bradley's own words:

"I was running low on time so I had to make some quick decisions. I wanted to at least attempt to block his bingo lane, but I also needed to set up a Q spot. . . . I laid down J2 FA 15, which would set up (F)AQIR 34 next turn, but then I realized it didn't block his lane at all. If he plays a 7 ending in S next turn, I'm screwed. NEG (3I, 4) seemed to be perfect, because it set up FAQIR for a zillion points, and would not likely be blocked, especially if he gets his bingo."

Given that Paul had just tacked an A onto ET for 3 points, it is clear that he was fishing for a bingo, or at the very least had the one remaining S. Bradley's play both forced Paul's bingo to be one that did not end in S and protected FAQIR from being blocked had Paul played the bingo. As it turned out, Paul bingoed with SINUATE and lost after Bradley's FAQIR play.

Example #17

You: 303 | Opponent: 324

Your rack: A B E H S S X

Solution: HEXOSANS (6H, 43). A nice play through three disconnected tiles.
HEXOSAN is about as good as HEXOSANS.

Example #18

You: 337 | Opponent: 387

Your rack: A E M P O O S

Solution: IPOMOEAS (14A, 109). There is nothing like a six-way overlap bingo play to brighten up the day. One almost needs a calculator to tally up the score.

Example #19

You: 142 | Opponent: 178

Your rack: D E P O R U V

Solution: LOUVERED (O8, 36). A nice eight-letter non-bingo play.

Example #20

You: 365 | Opponent: 352

Your rack: K M N

Unseen tiles: I L

Solution: AMI (11B, 9). This insightful defensive play saves the game by preventing the opponent from playing out with what would have been a fantastic play: WHIRLIGIG (A7).

Example #21

You: 342 | Opponent: 370

Your rack: B E I J N U X

Solution: BIJOU (3I, 34). This is a reconstruction of a club game in which I was a kibitzer rather than a player. At the time, I thought that BIJOUX was the best play, as it scores 16 additional points more than BIJOU does. It turns out that BIJOU is way better, because EX remains on the rack for VEX at N1 next turn, or VEXT if one of the two remaining T's is picked.

Example #22

You: 302 | Opponent: 391

Your rack: I R S T Y ☐ ☐

Opponent's last play: BELT (K8, 16)
Unseen tiles: A I L T U U U V V X

If opponent does not hold a truly horrid rack, then playing the bingo immediately with H<u>I</u>ST<u>O</u>RY (12I, 81) probably loses. Consequently, a win becomes more likely by doing something else.

There are at least four non-bingo plays all of which increase our winning chances versus playing a bingo right now. They are the one-tile plays of QANATS (H6, 15) and IS (10B, 9), and the two-tile plays of TYER (4I, 16) and MATERNALL<u>Y</u> (E2, 28), although I would rule out MATERNALL<u>Y</u> because it gives up a blank. To a certain extent, it doesn't matter which one we play, because opponent cannot empty the bag. He will let us do that, and the key point here is that when we do empty it, we had better have an unblockable bingo, or two bingos in places distant from each other. Thus there is no single best move in this position. However, a bingo should not be played.

The actual game was between Dave Wiegand and Adam Logan. Dave played H<u>I</u>ST<u>O</u>RY and won. Adam's rack was ILUUUVV.

Example #23

You: 221 | Opponent: 209

Your rack: A B E E H M Q

Solution: AHEM (1A, 56). The Canadian expert Albert Hahn once described the hook as the soul of SCRABBLE. I agree.

Example #24

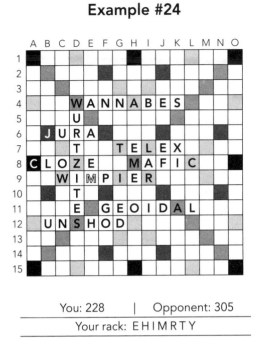

You: 228 | Opponent: 305

Your rack: E H I M R T Y

Solution: MYTHIER (5H, 103). A SCRABBLE bromide is *Find a good play, then look for a better one.* This position came from a club game that Gabriel Gauthier-Shalom played against me. He spotted THYMIER (13F, 87) quickly, took a breath, looked around the board, and there it was: MYTHIER for another 16 points!

Example #25

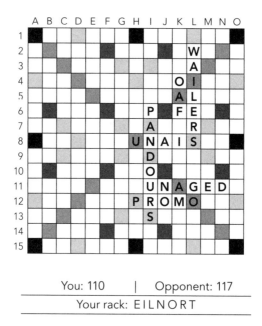

You: 110 | Opponent: 117

Your rack: E I L N O R T

Solution: TOILER (M1, 33). Great bingo-building letters, but on a closed board. This nice five-way overlap play is much superior to a fishing play.

Example #26

You: 26 | Opponent: 46

Your rack: A D F L R S Y

Solution: ROUGHDRY (8H, 48). A nice extension play.

Example #27

You: 384 | Opponent: 420

Your rack: B N O ☐

Opponent's rack: N N N O R

Solution: L<u>O</u>O (M1, 28). Playing out with BON<u>E</u> (4A, 24) loses by 2 points. But L<u>O</u>O, followed by BANG (6I, 14) or NAB (K11, 14) wins. Should opponent play OX (13G, 15), BIN (F13, 17) wins by 1.

Example #28

You: 313 | Opponent: 364

Your rack: E I R R R S T

Solution: TRISTE (O1, 41). I made this play in a game from the 2009 National SCRABBLE Championship, which I unfortunately lost anyway.

Example #29

You: 249 | Opponent: 323

Your rack: A A K N P R U

Solution: PAKORA (B10, 55). This play hooks the P in front of SHAW to create a nice high-scoring play.

Example #30

You: 22 | Opponent: 27

Your rack: A E G P R S T

Solution: GASPEREAUX (8A, 69). This magnificent front extension play was made by Marlon Hill in the 2009 National SCRABBLE Championship. Yes, Marlon could have played PARGETS (K9) for an extra 9 points. PARGETS simulates about 2 points better than GASPEREAUX. But GASPEREAUX is so surprising! And of course there is always a chance that a play like this might be challenged (it was not, in this instance).

Example #31

You: 405 | Opponent: 424

Your rack: A A I L S S

Opponent's rack: E M T

Solution: SALSA (13A, 41). Plays that hook the S onto KANJI (SISAL, LASSI, ASSAI, 35) all lose to opponent's MET (2M, 17). But the elegant triple-hook SALSA (13A, 41) wins by three.

Example #32

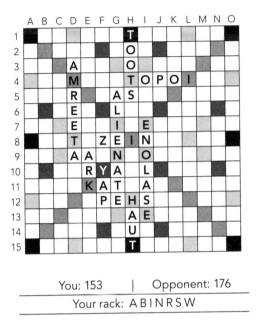

You: 153 | Opponent: 176

Your rack: A B I N R S W

Solution: RAINBOW (3C, 47). A nice play through two disconnected letters, and which makes good use of the three premium squares it covers.

Example #33

You: 201 | Opponent: 231

Your rack: B E E L M N R

Solution: LIMNER (E2, 38). From the same game, three moves later (RAINBOW wasn't played). LIMNER is a great four-way overlap.

Example #34

You: 409 | Opponent: 394

Your rack: A D E M N O R

Opponent's rack: A E I L M N T

Solution: RAMONA (M1, 39). A very nice inside hook play that wraps up the win.

Example #35

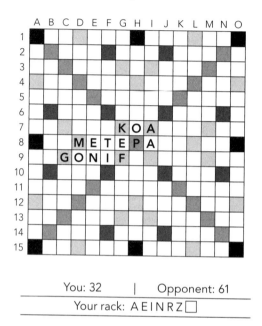

You: 32 | Opponent: 61

Your rack: A E I N R Z □

Solution: <u>H</u>ARMONIZE (D5, 88). The only bingo.

Example #36

You: 190 | Opponent: 174

Your rack: E F G H I L R

Solution: HIGHFLIER (5D, 80). From a little later in the same game. Once again, HIGHFLIER is the only bingo.

Example #37

You: 348 | Opponent: 387

Your rack: E I C N R S Y

Opponent's rack: A E I O R U V

Solution: PENDENCY (O1, 48). This extension play wins the game. Opponent played VIGA (F3, 21) afterward, and the first player then went out with SHRI (2G, 9).

How to Play SCRABBLE Like a Champion

Example #38

	A	B	C	D	E	F	G	H	I	J	K	L	M	N	O
1															
2								O	P						
3								H	A						
4								I	N						
5								A	T						
6									I						
7									E						
8				D	O	G	S								
9					U										
10	F			F	I	D									
11	A		Y	E		E									
12	V		O	R		A	R								
13	A	Z	U	K	I		L	I							
14				N		E	M								
15			Q	U	E	E	R								

You: 168 | Opponent: 140

Your rack: A E L N N T ☐

Solution: ANTENAT<u>A</u>L (5D, 82). Before the 2006 dictionary revision, opportunities for nine-letter plays occurred rarely, perhaps once every twenty games. Now they come up about three times as frequently.

Example #39

You: 361 | Opponent: 365

Your rack: E I D L R S T

Unseen tiles: A D E H J O R T V

Solution: DOLERITES (15E, 61). An alert bingo find, played through two disconnected letters.

Example #40

You: 340 | Opponent: 364

Your rack: A B C D E I ☐

Opponent's rack: D E I L T U

Solution: BI (9C, 14). We conclude this chapter with the most brilliant move that I have ever seen on a SCRABBLE board. Technically it is not even the best play, but that is a minor consideration, as you will see.

This position was reached in a game between Nigel Richards and Joey Mallick, played at the 2009 National SCRABBLE Championship. Nigel appeared to be in a lost position. However, his play of BI sets up an incredible out play: DECAGONAL (E3, 28). Joey can block the play with DEIL (6D, 18), but that loses to the easy out play of CADES (5A, 25) by one point. All other attempts to block DECAGONAL lose as well.

Could Nigel have won in a less spectacular fashion? BIDE (6B, 17) sets up ARC (A6, 20). But Joey can block that play with LITRE (F4, 17), after which QCA (9B, 14) loses by two points. BADE (6B, 17) loses to TIDED (D2, 14), and BICE (6B, 18) falls to LUETIC (D1, 16). CODEIA (6B, 27) is a blunder that loses immediately to DUCTILE (B4, 12).

All plays other than BI lose, except for AB (15N, 17). This play threatens DECIARE (F2, 13), which always wins if not blocked, except if Joey plays DUI (9B, 12). However, DUI allows Nigel to play out and win with a 15-point play from B4 to B10. I can't tell you what it is, because it isn't in the OSPD, only in the OWL.

In summary, both AB and BI win for Nigel. Nevertheless, BI was truly spectacular.

Appendix A

SCRABBLE Resources

Resources for the interested SCRABBLE player include study aids, computer-playing programs, organizations, and mailing lists. A comprehensive list of SCRABBLE resources can be found on the Internet at:

http://www.teleport.com/~stevena/scrabble/faqtext.html

Other sources of such information include the Wikipedia article on SCRABBLE:

http://en.wikipedia.org/wiki/Scrabble

as well as the National SCRABBLE Association website:

http://www2.scrabble-assoc.com/

and the North American SCRABBLE Players Association website:

http://www.scrabbleplayers.org/

Rather than repeat the information that can be found at these sites, I will simply present a subjective list of SCRABBLE resources that I think are must-haves. At the top of the list is Quackle, which of course I have referred to and relied upon heavily throughout this book. This amazing SCRABBLE playing program is free, though donations are welcome. It is available at:

http://people.csail.mit.edu/jasonkb/quackle/

A number of computer-based study programs have been developed over the years, but Zyzzyva is the only one currently available. It is excellent. You can also generate word lists from Zyzzyva, and it has also been used to adjudicate tournament SCRABBLE games. Like Quackle, Zyzzyva is free (donations welcome). It can be found at:

http://www.zyzzyva.net/

If you intend to play in sanctioned SCRABBLE tournaments in North America you will have to join the North American SCRABBLE Players Association (NASPA). NASPA is responsible for tournament and club

SCRABBLE in Canada and the United States. It produces online newsletters, processes memberships, regulates club play, takes responsibility for rules changes, calculates and publishes player ratings, and plans large tournaments and events such as the National SCRABBLE Championship:

http://www.scrabbleplayers.org/

There are a number of online sites for playing SCRABBLE. My two favorites are the official site run through Facebook by Electronic Arts:

http://apps.new.facebook.com/ea_scrabble_closed

and the Internet SCRABBLE Club:

http://www.isc.ro/

If you like to read about and discuss various SCRABBLE-related issues with about 1,200 like-minded fanatics, consider joining the Yahoo group crossword-games-pro. You must be a tournament player to join:

http://sasj.com/cgp

Go to Cross-Tables to check out performance histories of almost all North American tournament players, current rankings, listings of upcoming tournaments, and much more:

http://cross-tables.com/

The Last Word, run by Cornelia Guest, is an excellent online monthly magazine devoted to SCRABBLE:

http://www.thelastwordnewsletter.com/

Appendix B

The Basic Rules of SCRABBLE

EQUIPMENT: The equipment that makes up a SCRABBLE game consists of one hundred tiles, a tile bag, two to four tile racks, and the game board. Also needed are score sheets for each player and either the Official Word List (for tournament and club play) or the Official SCRABBLE Players Dictionary (for all other play).

Individual letters of the alphabet are printed on ninety-eight of the tiles, one letter to a tile. The other two tiles are blanks, and have the same function as jokers do in a deck of cards: the player can choose to make the blank any of the twenty-six letters. Printed on every lettered tile is a number that appears below and to the right of the letter. This number is the tile value of the letter (a blank has a tile value of zero). Tile values are essential for determining the number of points earned for a play.

A letter's tile value is determined by the frequency of usage of that letter in the language. The common letters A, E, I, O, U, L, N, R, S, and T are worth 1 point each. Less common letters such as F and V are worth 4 points each. The J and X are valued at 8 points, and the Q and Z are each worth 10. Low-value tiles predominate in the tile distribution, as they do in English language usage. There are twelve E's among the hundred tiles, but only one each of J, K, Q, X, and Z.

The board consists of a 15 × 15 matrix of squares. However, not all of the squares are alike. Some of them are shaded. These squares are called premium squares, and there are four varieties of them: double letter, triple letter, double word, and triple word. The double and triple letter squares used to be colored light blue and blue, respectively. The double and triple word squares were pink and red, respectively. Hasbro now makes a variety of SCRABBLE sets, and some of them no longer follow this color scheme.

The square at the center of the board is starred, and is a double word square.

Beginning the game

In order to start a game, each player draws one tile from the tile bag. The person who draws closer to the beginning of the alphabet goes first, with blanks taking precedence over A's. In the case of three or four players, play proceeds clockwise from the person who goes first. Most serious players refuse to play a game involving more than two players. There is too much luck involved, and the player who goes third or fourth is at a big disadvantage. The rules presented here deal solely with SCRABBLE as played by two people.

The player who goes first picks seven tiles and places them on the rack. The second player then does the same. Players are not permitted to look at each other's tiles. The first player begins the game by making a two- to seven-letter word from the tiles picked, and placing that word on the board. One letter must cover the star on the board, and the play may be made either vertically or horizontally. The first player may also begin by exchanging any or all of his tiles, or by simply passing his turn without exchanging tiles. Procedural details related to exchanging and passing are described in Chapter 2.

Allowable plays

Three criteria must be met for a play to be allowable. First, the tiles added to the board must all be on the same column or row. Second, they must either be placed adjacent to each other to form a word or be placed so that they combine with previously played tiles already on the column or row to create a word. Third, the tiles played must connect to tiles that have already been played. It *is* permissible to play only one tile from the rack, even if the sole purpose of the tile is to tack an -S onto a preexisting word.

HOW TO SCORE A PLAY: Plays are scored by adding up the tile values of the word formed. HOME is worth 9 points, for example. The tile values of its constituent letters are four, one, three, and one, which add up to nine. Of course, this score may be modified by the premium squares. For example, an opening play of QUEUE (8D) is worth 48 points: the Q falls on a double letter square and is thus worth 20 points. The other letters are worth 1 point each, so the play is worth $(20 + 1 + 1 + 1 + 1) \times 2$, or 48.

The value of a play that forms more than one new word is calculated by adding up the values of the individual new words formed.

Plays that use all seven tiles on the rack are called bingos and are worth the value of the play plus a bonus of 50 points.

This goes without saying, but I will add it anyway: the winner of the game is the player with the most points at the end of the game.

Index

About the Author

Joel Wapnick won the National (U.S.) SCRABBLE Championship in 1983, the Canadian SCRABBLE Championship in 1998, and the World SCRABBLE Championship in 1999. He finished second once and third twice in the Nationals and was runner-up twice in the Worlds. He teaches music at McGill University in Montreal and hopes one day to be better known as a novelist than as a SCRABBLE player.